SPIRITUAL GIFTS & THE CHURCH

DONALD BRIDGE
DAVID PHYPERS

INTER-VARSITY PRESS
DOWNERS GROVE
ILLINOIS 60515

© 1973 by
Inter-Varsity Press,
London.
Second American printing,
August 1974, by
InterVarsity Press with
permission from
Inter-Varsity Fellowship,
England.

InterVarsity Press
is the book publishing
division of Inter-Varsity
Christian Fellowship.

Quotations from the Bible
are from the
Revised Standard Version
(copyrighted 1946 and 1952,
Second Edition 1971, by the
Division of Christian Education,
National Council of the
Churches of Christ in the
United States of America),
unless otherwise stated.

ISBN: 0-87784-672-3
Library of Congress
Catalog Card
Number: 73-89303

Printed in the United
States of America

To Raymond and Elizabeth
who have helped us so much in our
growing understanding and
exercise of spiritual gifts

CONTENTS

PREFACE

'Spiritual gifts', 'speaking with tongues', the 'baptism of the Holy Spirit' – these topics, once largely the preserve of recognizable denominational groups, are all matters of active debate among Christians today. Few churches and few Christian groups in our colleges and universities have remained untouched by what many believe to be a resurgence of the spiritual gifts exercised in the early church. Across a remarkably broad spectrum of different church traditions during the past ten years the issue has been raised. Leaders of most denominations have found it necessary to express opinions, write articles, give advice, and (in some cases) speak out in approval or condemnation.

Here lies the painful problem. The reactions are so varied, and indeed so contradictory. Some Christians testify to undoubted blessing which has come into their lives following what they firmly believe to be the application of rediscovered New Testament teaching. So great is their own enthusiasm that they are puzzled by the reluctance of fellow-Christians to seek similar blessing for themselves. Yet those who hesitate are often as devout, as Bible-believing, and as eager for useful Christian service as those who hurry ahead. Some of them see grave theological difficulties. Others point to serious excesses and suspect an approach which can lead to such mistakes. All too easily both sides can take up extreme positions, and soon division appears amongst Christians who once worked happily together. Motives are doubted; experiences are questioned;

scriptural texts become ammunition in a war of words.

It is for the ordinary disciple of Christ, in church and Christian Union, perhaps excited or maybe puzzled by the current charismatic movement, that this book has been written. The writers, when the book began, were fellow church officers in a growing church. Their work also brought them into contact with students in senior schools and at college. The issues which are discussed in this book arose in the most practical way – through the need to evaluate the claims made by believers for whom they had pastoral responsibility, and through being involved in situations where the intervention of God was desperately needed. In that context, the Bible had to be searched again with a sincere desire to find what its teaching was, and with a firm determination to put each situation, each experience and each claim to the test of 'What saith the Lord?'.

This, then, is not a learned theological treatise for the academic specialist. Nor is it a collection of anecdotes (of which we could tell many). Nor is it a review of church history. On the other hand, right understanding is essential to correct practice. And while there are many areas of Scripture where united interpretation will probably never be reached, it has seemed to us that there are great fundamental truths which all serious Christians hold in common. It is to these basic truths that every experience and every practice must be faithful. Unless Christians can begin from the position of the need for regeneration (as in John 3), the deity of Christ (as in John 1), the sinner's sole dependence on the grace of God (as in Ephesians 2), the paramount need for holiness of life and the paramount importance of love (as in 1 Corinthians 13), then it is impossible for them to start a discussion on common ground.

Before long, however, the discussion takes us on to more debatable ground. Most Bible scholars will frankly admit that there are passages of Scripture whose interpretation is not easy. References which were clear to the original readers of, say, one of Paul's Epistles, are obscure to the twentieth-century reader. For example, whatever was the

8

'baptism for the dead' referred to in 1 Corinthians 15? There are no other references. A reverent guess is the best we can make. Similarly, the whole area of the pattern of church government is fraught with difficulties. One of the reasons for the existence of separate denominations today is the difficulty of being completely sure about this subject. Equally devout students come to different conclusions, and will probably admit that they could not avoid approaching their study with some personal and historical presuppositions. Another area of doubt is reached when we approach narrative portions of the Bible. Are we drawing the correct conclusion from the story? Is an incident recorded as a warning or as an example? If it is an example, is it normal or exceptional? Do the doctrinal passages throw light on the narrative? We shall return to this particular difficulty in our treatment of the middle section of the book. For the present, let us emphasize that there are understandable and legitimate differences of interpretation.

Because of this fact, a study of spiritual gifts must do two things. It must constantly return to biblical principles which are indisputable. And when it touches on more debatable subjects (such as, surely, the precise nature, classification and function of some of the gifts briefly mentioned in the New Testament), we must carefully compare whatever references are available, set them in their context and look cautiously for any light shed by church history or current experience. Having done so we can at least make a reverent suggestion in an attitude devoid of arrogant certainty or of harsh criticism.

Thus our book falls into three sections. We begin with a suggested approach to spiritual gifts in all their rich variety which sets them within the context of the church as the body of Christ. This raises topics which should be discussed and explored.

Secondly, we try to set teaching about 'the baptism of the Spirit' in an over-all New Testament context. We realize that here we shall not earn the approval of every reader. But surely we can share our convictions and if

9

necessary agree to disagree? After all, Christians do this with the subject of water-baptism.

Finally, we offer some practical suggestions, and the book ends as a plea for tolerance. God has given His Spirit and His gifts to unite, not to divide His church. It is our humble hope and prayer that in reading this book Christians of varied persuasions will approach this vital subject again with open minds and teachable hearts. We all have prejudices and fears which make this difficult. We all have precious experiences and deeply-held convictions which make it painful too! But the alternative is more difficult and more painful. The church in the closing decades of the twentieth century cannot afford to close its life to anything that God offers in the way of power and boldness. Nor can it afford to pursue fascinating by-roads which only exhaust its energies. Perhaps least of all can it afford to create new areas of division amongst those who love Christ and His gospel.

I SPIRITUAL GIFTS:
THEIR PLACE IN THE CHURCH

1 THE NATURE OF THE CHURCH

Mistaken views of the church

What is the church? Perhaps there is more confusion among Christians today about the answer to this question than has existed for a long time. For some, it is a visible religious organization, governed by a hierarchy of officials, which is the sole repository of religious truth and therefore able to pronounce on all matters of religious belief and behaviour covering every detail of human life. For others the church is little more than an efficient social agency, a caring community in a careless world, giving selflessly even to the point of losing its identity in meeting the needs of others. For others the church is a building at the end of the street, perhaps with a spire or a tower or maybe with a corrugated-iron roof. It is a useful place to hold ceremonies at the crucial points of life – birth, marriage and death – but its members are viewed as being a little odd and its ministers speak a language few can understand. For yet others the church is a social club, a place where useful and worthy activities are pursued including religious services on Sundays and other selected occasions. And even that does not exhaust all the possibilities.

While there may be some element of truth in each of the answers outlined above, the main drawback with all of them is that, pursued to their logical conclusion, all make the church no more than a human organization or agency. Anyone with sufficient daring and personal charm can claim to be the sole recipient of religious truth, gain a following and establish an organization to propagate his views. A glance at the agencies which exist to extend the views of Joseph Smith and Nathan H. Knorr is sufficient to establish this principle. Similarly any individual or group of people with a concern for the economic, cultural or intellectual problems of any of their fellow human beings can establish agencies to alleviate them. There need be no religious basis for their foundations, nor need criticism of their work necessarily be incurred thereby. Again, non-religious people may devise impressive ceremonies to cele-brate crucial experiences of life and there is ample evidence from many parts of the world of ways in which this has been done. Yet again, it is obvious that people may organize societies to provide for a multitude of human activities and sometimes these may include a religious element with no connection with Christianity or any major world religion.

The point is that if the church is nothing more than one or more, or even the sum, of the types of society outlined above, then it is no different from any other type of human society. On the other hand, if we are to accept the teaching of the New Testament we shall have to recognize that, while the church may exhibit some of the characteristics of other human societies, it is quite different from them all.

The body of Christ

When describing the church the New Testament writers frequently use the metaphor of a body, the body of Christ. Thus Christ is described as 'the head of the body, the church' (Col. 1: 18). Christians are told they are 'the body of Christ and individually members of it' (1 Cor. 12: 27). God is portrayed as having put all things under the feet of Christ, 'and has made him the head over all things for the church, which is his body, the fulness of him who fills all in all' (Eph. 1: 22, 23).

The use of this metaphor is important because it signifies that the church is more than a human organization; it is a living organism. It is a body whose Head is Christ and whose members are individual Christians. Indeed it is a supernatural body for, unlike natural organisms, it is not subject to death. Its Head, Christ, is alive for evermore (Rev. 1: 18), and its members too through their faith in the Head will never die (Jn. 11: 26). Thus, unlike other human societies, the church cannot be destroyed (Mt. 16: 18). Although it may at certain times possess some visible organization, if this organization is disbanded and suppressed the church lives on. This has happened, for example, in Communist China and a book can be published about it entitled *The Chinese Church That Will Not Die*. Again, although the church may possess its own property, if its buildings are closed or destroyed (as, for example, has occurred over wide areas of the Soviet Union) then the church survives, indeed grows, as Christians continue to meet for worship in their homes, in the countryside and maybe even in prison together. When Christians are hunted down, tortured and executed for their faith in Christ, still the church marches on; for 'the blood of the martyrs is the seed of the church'.

This supernatural character of the church needs particular assertion at the present time, for many are denying it even from within the church's own ranks. The whole tenor of current secular theology, theology supposedly for 'man come of age', is directed towards removing all traces of the supernatural from Christian thinking. Thus the miracles of Jesus and the reality of His bodily resurrection are denied; the need for a saving change in the human heart is similarly questioned. Discovery of God is reduced to discovery of oneself, and the living, supernatural God of Scripture is pronounced dead.

This sort of thing is not new, of course. So important is it to the church's vitality for Christians to realize its supernatural character that from time to time the adversary attempts to deny it or obscure it. In the eighteenth century the church's supernatural character was denied by the teachings of the Deists with their reduction of God to a distant First Cause now no longer interested in His universe and only worthy of worship through 'natural religion'. Earlier still Arianism and Gnosticism, if triumphant, would have similarly destroyed the church's supernatural character, by accommodating its life and teaching to the passing philosophies of their time.

However learned and impressive the reasoning of modern theologians may be, fidelity to Scripture demands that Christians recognize the supernatural character of their faith. Christians worship a supernatural sovereign God, 'who accomplishes all things according to the counsel of his will' (Eph. 1: 11). Christians believe in a supernatural divine intervention in human history in the person of God's beloved Son, born of a virgin (Mt. 1), 'attested . . . by God with mighty works and wonders and signs which God did through him' (Acts 2: 22), presented alive to His disciples 'after his passion by many proofs' (Acts 1: 3), now at the right hand of the throne of God on high where He always lives to make intercession for those who draw near to God through Him (Heb. 7: 25). Christians possess in Holy Scripture a supernatural revelation of the character and work of God on their behalf because 'no prophecy ever came by the impulse of man, but men moved by the Holy Spirit spoke from God' (2 Pet. 1: 21). Christians are the product of a supernatural change in their hearts whereby, from being dead in their trespasses and sins, they have been made alive together with Christ (Eph. 2: 1, 5). As a result they are expected to display a supernatural character of love which far transcends mere human courtesy or affection (1 Cor. 13). Christians are part, as has been shown, of a supernatural organism, the church, divinely established on the day of Pentecost through the gift of the Holy Spirit (Acts 2). Through their membership of the body of Christ Christians enjoy supernatural endowments, spiritual gifts, to enable them to continue the work of Christ in the world (Eph. 4), and their spiritual life is nourished so that they increase in holiness (1 Pet. 2). Christians are looking forward to a supernatural climax to human history when Christ will return and their salvation will be complete (1 Thes. 4).

Every cardinal Christian doctrine taught in Scripture thus implies the intervention of God, the bursting in of the transcendent, the spiritual, the divine – and Christianity cannot be explained or lived if this is forgotten or denied. We are living at a time when even Christians who have paid lip-service to the supernatural character of their faith have often largely denied it in practice. Could it be that, through a rediscovery of genuine spiritual gifts, God is beginning to lead His people back to a rediscovery of the power available to them through faith in Himself? Or is the church in danger of plunging into a pursuit of the subjective, the emotional, the merely colourful, as an escape from the stern demands made on it by modern life?

2 SPIRITUAL GIFTS WITHIN THE CHURCH

The purpose of spiritual gifts

It is particularly important that Christians should be clear in their minds about scriptural teaching on the nature of the church before examining what the Bible says about the nature of spiritual gifts, for on the three occasions when Paul deals with gifts in his letters he always does so within the context of teaching about the church. In Romans 12 Paul first describes the church as the body of Christ and Christians as individual members of it (verses 4, 5) before listing different gifts which Christians exercise as a result (verses 6–8). In his more extended treatment of gifts in 1 Corinthians 12–14 his reasoning is identical. 'Now you are the body of Christ and individually members of it. And God has appointed in the church first apostles, second prophets . . . ' (1 Cor. 12: 27, 28). Similarly in Ephesians 4 Paul reasons that it is because Christians are members of one body that grace has been given to each of them according to the measure of Christ's gift (verses 1–8).

Closer examination of these three passages reveals that gifts play a vital, twofold purpose in the life of the church. First, they strengthen the church's fellowship. God's will for the church is, 'that there may be no discord in the body, but that the members may have the same care for one another. If one member suffers, all suffer together; if one member is honoured, all rejoice together' (1 Cor. 12: 25, 26). Gifts are variously distributed among church members that this end might be realized (1 Cor. 12: 27–30). Thus in their desire for, and exercise of, manifestations of the Spirit Christians should 'strive to excel in building up the church' (1 Cor. 14: 12). Similarly in Ephesians 4 Paul reasons that Christ's gifts were 'for building up the body of Christ' (verse 12), and he concludes that, when each part of the body is working properly, that is, when Christians are rightly exercising their various gifts, then the church 'makes bodily growth and upbuilds itself in love' (verse 16).

Secondly, besides strengthening the church's fellowship, spiritual gifts extend the church's witness and ministry. In admittedly difficult verses in 1 Corinthians 14: 20–25 Paul appears to reason that the manifestation of intelligible spiritual gifts will convict the unbeliever of his sin so that, 'falling on his face, he will worship God and declare that God is really among you' (1 Cor. 14: 25). Rather more clearly in Ephesians 4 Paul declares that gifts are for the equipment of the saints and the work of ministry, and significantly, in the same context, he specifically recognizes the offices of apostle and evangelist (verses 11, 12).

The practical outworking of this principle is of course seen most clearly in the narratives of the Acts of the Apostles. The initial manifestation of the Spirit on the day of Pentecost followed by Peter's Spirit-filled preaching brought three thousand new members into the church (Acts 2: 41). The regular wonders and signs done through the apostles (Acts 2: 43) meant that day by day the Lord added to the church those who were being saved (Acts 2: 47). The healing of the lame man at the Beautiful Gate of the Temple and subsequent preaching by Peter brought the number of Christian men in Jerusalem to about five thousand (Acts 4: 4). Peter's exercise of the gift of knowledge enabling him to expose the deception of Ananias and Sapphira resulted in more believers than ever being added to the Lord, 'multitudes both of men and women' (Acts 5: 14). The martyrdom of Stephen led to evangelism in Samaria, and, a little later, to the conversion of Saul. And so the connection continued. Because so many members of the early church were keen to exercise all the gifts that were available to them, that church grew and was strong.

The importance of understanding the place of spiritual gifts within the life and witness of the church as a whole cannot be overstressed, for when this is done their value for others, rather than for the individual Christian exercising them, is emphasized. Regrettably this emphasis has not always been made by some who have ardently encouraged others to seek various gifts. Some gifts have been pressed on fellow Christians because of the personal thrill which is said to accompany their exercise. Other gifts have been regarded as rewards for personal holiness and dedication. In some circles the presence or absence of gifts has been used as a yardstick to measure individual Christians' progress in their faith. Now, of course, exercising spiritual gifts may well be thrilling, for all service for Christ brings its own deep satisfaction. And those whose lives are deeply dedicated to Christ and who are displaying the fruits of the Spirit in their lives (see Gal. 5: 22, 23) may well find that God richly endows them with many of the spiritual gifts about which Scripture speaks. But no necessary connection between personal thrills and holy lives and the exercise of gifts is made in Paul's letters, and the passages considered at the beginning of this chapter never suggest that the presence or absence of gifts can be used as a yardstick to measure spirituality. 'Strive to excel in building up the church' is Paul's advice to those 'eager for manifestations of the Spirit' (1 Cor. 14: 12). We feel that had this emphasis been more clearly stressed in recent times many of the abuses and excesses which have sometimes characterized the exercise of gifts might well have been avoided.

The nature of spiritual gifts

In 1 Corinthians 12 the apostle Paul deals in some depth with the nature of spiritual gifts. He uses a number of different Greek words to describe them and a systematic study of these is particularly rewarding.

First, in verse 1, Paul uses the word *pneumatikoi* to describe the gifts. Usually translated 'spiritual gifts', a more literal translation of the word would be 'spiritual things' or, more simply, 'spirituals'. It is derived from *pneuma*, another Greek word used in Scripture to describe the Holy Spirit of God, and the use of *pneumatikoi* to describe the gifts shows that they belong to and are actuated by the Holy Spirit and thus cannot find their explanation solely in terms of natural ability. Does this imply, then, that they are always spectacular, always mysterious?

The word certainly does not demand such a meaning. But it does seem to imply that the *initiative* is with the Holy Spirit. Whether it be an endowment outside normal experience, or a talent which may seem quite natural, its exercise springs from the instigation and activity of God. Because God wishes to communicate His will, a 'prophecy' is given. Because God desires the needy to be helped, a Christian is moved to perform an 'act of mercy'. Because God wishes the whole congregation to be edified, an 'interpretation' is granted. Because God is concerned for the orderly governing of the churches, abilities of leadership are granted. Because God reaches out in saving grace, the evangelist is given a message that is not of his own invention, with a power of persuasion that is not in his own personality. And because it is God the Holy Spirit who specifically works in these areas, the resulting endowments are called *pneumatikoi*. So Paul insists that all the gifts 'are inspired by one and the same Spirit' (1 Cor. 12: 11). It is surely because He inspires them, not because we consider them to be more or less unusual, that they are supernatural.

From *pneumatikoi* in verse 1 Paul moves to *charismata* in verse 4 in his description of 'the spirituals'. Often translated simply 'gifts', the term 'gifts of grace' more accurately denotes the meaning of the Greek word. Its use underlines the fact that gifts come from the free bounty of God's love and mercy and are not (contrary to the ideas of some, already outlined) rewards for service, or holiness or sincerity or maturity or anything else. Holiness and maturity may often be associated with the exercise of gifts, but God may sometimes display His sovereignty and grace by endowing quite young and inexperienced Christians with quite startling gifts for a particular purpose, and older Christians then have to beware lest they quench the Spirit by failing to recognize that God is at work. No Christian needs to possess an aura of 'holiness' or maturity before he can contribute to the enrichment of the church.

Charisma, the singular of *charismata*, is often used elsewhere in the New Testament to describe a gift of God's grace. In particular it is used in Romans 6: 23 to describe the gift of eternal life through Jesus Christ. This is God's greatest gift, effected through the miracle of regeneration. It is this gift which may be described as the gateway to all God's other gifts. Possession of eternal life is essential before any of the other gifts can be truly exercised. Nor can any other gift exceed this fundamental gift of regeneration in its miraculous, supernatural and divinely-stamped qualities.

The third word Paul uses in 1 Corinthians 12 to describe spiritual gifts is *diakonia* (verse 5). The word, translated 'service', is used in the New Testament to describe the office and work of a 'deacon' or any kind of service or ministry in the church. It is a further reminder of the truth that gifts are to be exercised for the well-being of others and not for the bolstering or encouragement of oneself. The related verb *diakoneō* is used by Jesus in Mark 10: 45 where, speaking of Himself, He says, 'the Son of man also came not to be served but to serve, and to give his life as a ransom for many'. Thus the example of the Christian who exercises gifts must be the Saviour Himself in His death on the cross, and the Christian must always remember that God measures greatness not by the number of His gifts but by the willing, humble service for others of those who follow Him.

Next, Paul uses the word *energēma* translated 'working' (verse 6) to describe spiritual gifts. This Greek word is used in the New Testament only here and in verse 10. It is derived from the verb *energeō* which, in its passive form, means to be actuated or set in operation and in the New Testament is 'always used of some principle or power at work'.[1] It is this idea of power which is particularly appropriate to Paul's argument at this point for, when describing different gifts as 'varieties of working', he says 'it is the same God who inspires them all in every one'. Thus Paul is saying that, when gifts are exercised, God's power is at work in the Christian for the benefit of others. It is this sovereign activity of God in the life of the Christian which must always be remembered by those who exercise various gifts. Because God is sovereign He may withdraw gifts just as He has previously granted them. No Christian is permanently endowed with any gift. Indeed there are examples in Scripture of gifts being withdrawn or being granted only occasionally. Thus John the Baptist obviously exercised the gift of prophecy for a while yet wisely recognized that his gift was being withdrawn as the commencement of Jesus' public ministry approached. 'He must increase, but I must decrease' (Jn. 3: 30) was his wise and humble comment in the circumstances. Similarly, the apostle Paul seems to have exercised such gifts as healing and discerning of spirits only when confronted in a special way by those who were sick or possessed as, for example, the case of the lame man at Lystra (see Acts 14: 8–10), or the case of the slave-girl at Philippi (see Acts 16: 16–18). Paul never claimed to possess these gifts; he used them as occasion demanded.

The final word Paul employs to describe the nature of gifts is *phanerōsis* (verse 7). To each Christian, he says, is given the 'manifestation' of the Spirit for the common good. Like *energēma* this word is used only once elsewhere in the New Testament in 2 Corinthians 4: 2, where Paul uses it to describe the 'open statement' of the truth involved in the preaching of the gospel. The word is derived from the verb *phaneroein* which means to make visible or clear or known. Gifts are 'manifestations of the Spirit'; hence, when they are

[1] H. A. W. Meyer, *Critical and Exegetical Commentary on the New Testament* (T. and T. Clark, 1883).

exercised, God's nature or His way of dealing with men and women is made clear where there was ignorance or confusion before. It is important to grasp this, for on many occasions when gifts have been supposedly exercised in recent times they have left Christians divided and confused. Yet this should not be so and when confusion does result from the exercise of gifts Christians may be justified in asking whether they have been truly 'manifestations of the Spirit' or not.

The origin of gifts

The divine origin of spiritual gifts has been implicitly and continually recognized so far in this book. Indeed we have suggested that it is this that makes them supernatural. But it is instructive to notice how, in the verses in 1 Corinthians 12 under detailed consideration above, Paul associates each member of the Trinity in the origin and distribution of the gifts. Thus Paul writes, 'there are varieties of gifts, but the same *Spirit*; and there are varieties of service, but the same *Lord*; and there are varieties of working, but it is the same *God* who inspires them all in every one.' Particularly impressive is the way each Person of the Godhead is associated with different aspects of the gifts. Thus, since it is the special activity of the Holy Spirit to distribute, Paul speaks of His 'gifts'. As Jesus came not to be served but to serve, Paul speaks of His 'varieties of service'. Because God the Father is the source of all power, so Paul speaks of His 'varieties of working'. What tremendous activity, therefore, is encompassed in the exercise of spiritual gifts! When gifts are used by a member of the body of Christ then the whole Trinity is at work in one individual for the well-being and blessing of others!

The number of spiritual gifts

Much injustice has been done to New Testament teaching on gifts, even by some of their most ardent advocates, by the practice of referring to 'the nine gifts' as if only nine gifts of the Spirit exist. Nine are indeed listed in 1 Corinthians 12: 8–10 but Paul gives other lists of gifts at the end of the same chapter, in Romans 12 and in Ephesians 4, and he appears to describe more gifts in other separate passages. Not only is the New Testament total of gifts surprisingly large, but we are clearly making a big mistake if we think of them as always being dramatic, colourful and mysterious. Romans 12 lists prophecy, teaching, exhorting, liberal contribution, the giving of aid and acts of mercy. 1 Corinthians 12 lists the utterance of wisdom, the utterance of knowledge, faith, healing, the working of miracles, prophecy, the ability to distinguish between spirits, various kinds of tongues, the interpretation of tongues, apostles, teachers, helpers and administrators. Ephesians 4 speaks of the office rather than the activity, and presents us with apostles, prophets, evangelists, pastors and teachers. In addition, we shall reason later that voluntary celibacy (1 Cor. 7), voluntary poverty and martyrdom (1 Cor. 13: 3) are gifts in the same sense as all the others and need to be added to the total list.

It is tempting to subdivide the various gifts. There are the obviously miraculous (healing or tongues) and the surprisingly 'natural' (teaching or serving). There are the verbal (prophecy or interpretation), the mental (knowledge or discerning of spirits), the powerful (working of miracles), and the administrational (service or giving of aid). There are those gifts exercised by church officers recognized in every denomination and group (pastors) and those whose very meaning and existence today are keenly debated (apostleship or speaking with tongues). But what must be grasped is that, startling or ordinary, controversial or universally accepted, *all* of these gifts are in fact referred to as *charisma* and *all* are set within exactly the same context of the working of the body of Christ, the activity of the Spirit of God. For a church or group of Christians to concentrate on a limited number of gifts, forgetting the great variety presented by the New Testament, will inevitably result in a partial and incomplete ministry on their part with consequent loss of blessing both inside and outside the fellowship.

The permanence of spiritual gifts

Because some spiritual gifts are more obviously supernatural and miraculous than others, and because the exercise of these gifts has sometimes fallen into disuse for long periods during the church's history, some writers, while recognizing the essentially divine nature of the gospel and the church, have reasoned that these 'super-supernatural' gifts have passed out of use completely and should not be sought by present-day Christians. They maintain that such gifts were intended by God to be at the church's disposal only during the apostolic age, and were then withdrawn.

Taking as their starting-place the nature of apostleship (at least as exercised by the Twelve and by Paul) those who hold this view reason that, by its very nature, this gift was a temporary one. Its requirement that an apostle should be an eye-witness of the resurrection was impossible after the first generation of Christians had passed away. The special inspiration of the Holy Spirit granted for the writing of the New Testament Scriptures was similarly restricted to one generation. Thus apostleship constituted a 'foundation-gift'.

The argument then builds on this principle. Prophets were necessary only until the canon of Scripture was complete. Evangelists were the special delegates of the apostles. Thus, of the four gifts in Ephesians 4 only the pastor-teacher remains – the 'minister' of Reformed Christianity. In the same way the dramatic gifts listed in 1 Corinthians 12 are dealt with. These, so it is reasoned, were the necessary accompaniment to a foundation-ministry. Their miraculous exercise is typical of the occasional breaking-in of the obviously supernatural, variously described in Scripture as occurring at certain critical and epoch-making periods in the history of God's people such as the Exodus, the conquest of Canaan and the earliest prophetic ministries of Elijah and Elisha. The startling and visible manifestation in 'signs and wonders' was the divine authentication of the next step in God's purposes. It constituted a part of redemptive history (the once-for-all and completed acts of God for our redemption) rather than a part of church history (the ongoing and normative experience of God's people).

The argument is a sober and impressive one. It has a pedigree beginning with John Calvin and reaching its most classic expression with Benjamin Warfield. Some of its modern advocates believe that it virtually closes the discussion, and regard any claim for modern spiritual gifts to be based on the counterfeit.

But does the theory cope satisfactorily with all the facts of Scripture? Many Christians, thoroughly 'reformed' in other respects, are uneasy with it. It is an argument which begins with Scripture (the nature of apostleship) but quickly moves into the realm of deduction from Scripture. It takes no account of the fact that the Bible nowhere states that any of the gifts have passed away. Nor does the Bible suggest that it was only in apostolic times that the gospel required divine authentication with 'signs and wonders'. Nor does it in fact distinguish between the dramatic and the less dramatic gifts: as we have shown, all are set within the permanent framework of the nature of the church as the body of Christ. The gift of wisdom is placed beside the gifts of healing (1 Cor. 12: 8, 10). The exercise of prophecy is placed beside the giving of aid (Rom. 12: 6–8). The office of evangelist is listed with that of pastor-teacher (Eph. 4: 11). Helpers and administrators are addressed with those who speak in tongues (1 Cor. 12: 28). Why, if the two types of gifts are fundamentally different in character, does not Paul give them separate treatment instead of mixing them indiscriminately?

The gift-withdrawal theory also poses a problem to those who wish to use the New Testament as their handbook for the church. The only narrative they have to guide them is that supplied in the Acts of the Apostles. What that shows is a church living in the realm of the supernatural. 'Ordinary preaching' is mixed inextricably with miracles of healing. Common-sense decisions like the appointment of deacons to 'serve at tables' stand shoulder-to-shoulder with divine directions from angels and from the Holy Spirit. An 'ordinary' prayer-meeting leads to a miraculous rescue from prison. The two strands cannot be separated without destroying the whole. If one strand is not applicable today, the account ceases to be a guide in our situation and becomes only of historical interest. And we have nothing with which to replace it.

The same applies, though to a lesser extent, when attention is turned to the Epistles. True, most of them make no reference at all to charismatic gifts. They are concerned primarily with sound doctrine and holy living – as all Christians should be. But when they do touch on the subject of the exercise of gifts, they tell their readers how to regulate them, how to test them, how to recognize them, how to exercise them – never how to phase them out. The Epistle which regulates the observance of the Lord's Supper also regulates the exercise of charismatic gifts, with no suggestion that one or the other should cease. The Epistle which says, 'let a man examine himself, and so eat of the bread', also says, 'earnestly desire to prophesy, and do not forbid speaking in tongues'. Again, the only actual biblical instruction available on the subject assumes the presence of the gifts.

Paul does, of course, say that 'prophecies, they will pass away . . . tongues, they will cease . . . knowledge, it will pass away' (1 Cor. 13: 8), and this verse is often quoted to underline the temporary nature of dramatic gifts. But the context must be noted. Paul is speaking of the time when 'the perfect comes'; it is then that 'the imperfect will pass away' (verse 10). Similarly, he speaks of seeing now dimly, but then face to face, of knowing now in part but then understanding fully (verse 12). Clearly Paul is looking forward to a time yet future when not only colourful spiritual gifts but virtually everything that makes up normal life will have passed away in the final glorious fulfilment of the promises of God. This can have nothing to do with the passing of the apostolic age.

It seems, then, that the idea of gifts being withdrawn from the church at the end of the first century is not in itself capable of scriptural proof: it is a deduction or conclusion rightly or wrongly drawn from certain Scriptures but lacking clear scriptural statement itself. It represents an attempt to explain the gradual decline in supernatural activity which did in fact become apparent in the second, third and fourth centuries. Such a decline undeniably took place, though some writers are now suggesting that it was not so widespread and consistent as is usually supposed. There is, however, more than one possible explanation for it. During the same period the church's spiritual vitality as a whole declined. Its faithfulness to the apostolic gospel was not complete. Its distinctive life as a body of people separated unto God was compromised. As long as persecution continued the process was not rapid. After the imperial recognition of Christianity and its virtual adoption as the State religion, the process gathered speed. That much evidence of God's intervention disappeared at the same time is not surprising. Could not the cause and effect be here? It is at least thought-provoking that Tertullian was won over from the orthodox Christianity of the Western church to a protest and reform movement which linked together a return to apostolic purity and a revival of charismatic gifts.

This brief look at church history raises a further line of reasoning. Evangelical Christians believe that the church must be continually tested and reformed by the Word of God. The question must always be, not 'do we have a respectable lineage?' but 'are we now faithful to the apostolic doctrine and practice?' Such a question, when posed in the sixteenth century, precipitated the Protestant

Reformation. But if, as the Reformers believed, it had become possible for much of the apostles' life and doctrine to be lost by the church, could it not be at least possible that the charismatic had been lost too? If the church needed to recover New Testament teaching might it not need to recover the practices described in the New Testament? There is some evidence that the 'grandsons of the Reformation' – the Anabaptists – did so. It is not surprising that main-line Protestantism, reacting sharply from the crude religious magic of the medieval church, became suspicious of anything mysterious or miraculous, and turned its face against a revival of the apostolic gifts.

In considering the theory that God has withdrawn the 'super-supernatural' gifts from the life of the church we have tried to show that at best this is a respectable and thoughtful objection to the exercise of these gifts, but that it creates as many problems as it solves. It compels its exponents to go further than Scripture clearly goes. It interprets some historical events in a manner open to question. It requires the dismissal as counterfeit of some of the experiences of sincere and godly Christians today who can offer evidence in their own lives and ministries of the renewal of spiritual gifts. And perhaps most unfortunately, it creates an artificial division (as sadly its opposite view often does) between gifts dramatic and less dramatic which God has given for the functioning and growth and expansion of the Christian church. If *all* of the gifts, in the sense suggested earlier, are appointed by God for the healthy exercise and edifying of the church, is there not room for a careful and cautious exercise of them all, and a hearty recognition of the equally important place of them all in the twentieth century?

Indeed, as the century draws towards its close, the church would seem to need the benefits of spiritual gifts more than ever before. For at a time when Christians of all traditions realize deeply the imperfections of the church, Christ has given gifts 'for the perfecting of the saints' (Eph. 4: 12, AV). At a time when the continued existence of the Christian ministry is at stake, with panic, uncertainty and surrender on every hand, there are gifts 'for the work of ministry' (Eph. 4: 12). At a time when Christians are ashamed at their divisions but embarrassed by misdirected efforts to heal them, gifts are available 'until we all attain to the unity of the faith' (Eph. 4: 13). At a time when heresy and half-truth and doctrines of men bewilder Christians, God has given His gifts, 'so that we may no longer be children, tossed to and fro and carried about with every wind of doctrine, by the cunning of men, by their craftiness in deceitful wiles. Rather, speaking the truth in love, we are to grow up in every way into him who is the head, into Christ' (Eph. 4: 14, 15).

In the darkness and gloom so characteristic of much of the present-day Western church, spiritual gifts are being claimed by Christians in many different traditions, sometimes in the most unusual of places. Can this be an indication that God has not abandoned His people in these bewildering and depressing days?

3 GIFTS FOR RECOGNIZED CHURCH OFFICERS

When any attempt is made to apply New Testament teaching on the subject of spiritual gifts to the present-day situation certain problems immediately present themselves.

First, there is the problem of knowing precisely what the New Testament writers were describing when they wrote about the various gifts. Can we really be sure today that we know what Paul meant when, for example, we read about the 'utterance of knowledge'? If a group of Corinthian Christians could be translated to a twentieth-century 'charismatic' meeting would they recognize their exercise of 'speaking in tongues' as synonymous with what they might hear, and would their exercise of the interpretation of tongues correspond to modern practice? This, of course, is not a problem confined solely to the subject of spiritual gifts. It is present in many other areas of Christian understanding as well. How did New Testament Christians really celebrate the Lord's Supper? Did the early church always baptize by immersion, or were other modes admissible, if, for example, a baptism occurred in the early hours of the morning (see Acts 16: 33)? And when whole families were baptized (see Acts 16: 33; 1 Cor. 1: 16) were the children baptized along with the adults or not? How, precisely, were New Testament churches governed, and what authority, if any, did Christian leaders in one town have over Christian congregations in other towns?

While the lack of final answers to these and other

questions should not deter Christians from a reverent study of the Scriptures and from a ready willingness to obey the injunction earnestly to desire the spiritual gifts, it should always encourage a spirit of humility in this difficult area of understanding. Of all Christian knowledge Paul says that even he knows only in part (1 Cor. 13: 12), and if the knowledge of one through whom God gave some of the Scriptures was partial, how much more partial will be the understanding of those who hesitantly seek to follow in his footsteps?

A related problem to the difficulty of knowing precisely what the New Testament writers meant by the different *charismata* lies in the fact that several of the gifts appear to overlap each other. What, for example, is the difference between the giving of aid and the doing of acts of mercy? Does a prophet also exercise the utterance of wisdom, or knowledge? Does a teacher never prophesy, or evangelize? Does an evangelist exercise the gift of faith? Paul the apostle also exercised among others the gifts of tongues (1 Cor. 14: 18), the discerning of spirits (Acts 16: 18) and healing. While some gifts are obviously clear-cut, Scripture does not always place them into neat categories, and while we shall later attempt to describe the various gifts in turn, this fact must always be remembered and borne in mind by those who seek to exercise what God has for them.

A further problem in this area of understanding lies in the fact, already noted, that sometimes Scripture describes the gifts themselves (1 Cor. 12: 8–10) while at other times it lists the individuals who exercise the gifts (Eph. 4: 11). This is a problem because it raises the issue of church government. Does the New Testament suggest that all churches should have their specifically appointed apostles, prophets, evangelists, pastors and teachers, helpers and administrators? If so, few churches today would appear to be faithful to the New Testament norm, and any attempt to recreate such a norm would result only in the foundation of yet another denomination which would probably founder on the rocks of the worst kind of exclusivism and further division

33

within itself. Yet if all the gifts are to be exercised how can such a result be avoided?

Scripture itself seems to allow different forms of church government. The church at Jerusalem was governed by the apostles with help from the deacons and ratification of important decisions by the whole congregation (Acts 15: 22). The church at Antioch was ruled by prophets and teachers (Acts 13: 1). The churches in Asia Minor were in the care of elders appointed by Paul (Acts 14: 23). The leaders of the church at Philippi are described as 'bishops and deacons' (Phil. 1: 1) while Timothy and Titus appear to have had oversight over groups of churches somewhat after the fashion of a modern bishop.

In view of all this it would appear that Scripture demands that, within different frameworks of church officers, individuals should have the freedom to exercise the various gifts described in the New Testament. Some of these gifts will come to reside quite naturally in clearly recognizable individuals; others will be distributed more widely and perhaps more occasionally among the total number of God's people. Bearing this in mind we pass to a detailed consideration of those gifts which are specifically associated with officers in the church.

Apostles

We noted in the previous chapter how many biblical scholars have reasoned that the gift of apostleship was temporary only, because of the special position of the Twelve plus Paul in the early church.[1] Undoubtedly these were apostles in a very special sense with an unrepeatable rôle to play in the foundation of the church. They were variously qualified for their position by virtue of the fact that they had accompanied Jesus throughout His earthly ministry from His baptism to His ascension (Acts 1: 21, 22), that they had

[1] For a good statement of this view, see J. R. W. Stott, *The Preacher's Portrait* (Tyndale Press, 1961), pp. 11f.

seen the risen Lord and could therefore witness to His resurrection (Acts 1: 22; Gal. 1: 16; 1 Cor. 15: 8), and that their lives and witness bore the signs of true apostles (2 Cor. 12: 12). In the early church they regulated Christian doctrine and presided over the church's worship (Acts 2: 42). They bore responsibility for the admission of new groups into the fellowship of the church (Acts 8, 10, 11) and some of them, though not as many as asserted in tradition, played a leading rôle in taking the gospel to others (see Acts 1: 8; Gal. 2: 7). Because of their particular relationship with the Lord and because death, in time, brought to an end all their lives, and because the number of those who might possibly fulfil the qualifications outlined above was similarly limited to the length of human life, the apostleship of the Twelve plus Paul was necessarily temporary. But to conclude from this, as some have done, that the gift of apostleship was itself therefore temporary is surely to take the argument too far, as we showed earlier.[2]

First, although it is obvious that the New Testament does speak of the Twelve and Paul as apostles in a special sense, it describes many others as apostles as well. In 1 Corinthians 15 Paul seems to distinguish between 'the twelve' (verse 5) and 'all the apostles' (verse 7). In Galatians 1: 19 and 2: 9 James the Lord's brother is described as an apostle and is associated with Peter and John as a pillar of the church, yet he was not one of the Lord's disciples (see Jn. 7: 5). In Acts 14: 14 and 1 Corinthians 9: 5, 6 Barnabas is described as an apostle and in both instances no distinction is drawn between the nature of his apostleship and that of Paul and Peter. In Romans 16: 7 Andronicus and Junias are described as 'men of note among the apostles' while in 1 Thessalonians 2: 6 Silas and Timothy appear to be so described. While some of these such as James the Lord's brother might have qualified as apostles in the special sense outlined above by virtue of a resurrection appearance (see 1 Cor. 15: 7) and while others might have similarly qualified by being among the five hundred brethren to whom the risen Lord appeared

[2] See pp. 26ff.

(1 Cor. 15: 6), such a conclusion is by no means obvious and in the case of Timothy is inconceivable. Indeed the inescapable conclusion of these verses plus the recorded claim of false teachers to be 'apostles of Christ' (2 Cor. 11: 13) is that many besides the Twelve and Paul exercised the gift of apostleship in the early church and their gift was widely recognized. Indeed, the word simply means 'messenger' or 'delegate', and was widely used in that sense amongst the Jewish synagogues in which the gospel found its first hearers.

When the functions of apostles are more closely considered it becomes clearly evident that there is a continuing need for Christians who exercise this gift. Attention was drawn earlier to the twelve apostles' rôle in the regulation of the Christian faith (Acts 2: 42). By his many letters to early Christian congregations the apostle Paul clearly saw the regulation of their faith as part of his function too and was quick to assert the divine origin of his teaching when this was challenged (see Gal. 1: 11, 12). In one sense this apostolic function was temporary and came to an end with the conclusion of the New Testament. Thus Paul can describe the church as being 'built upon the foundation of the apostles and prophets' (Eph. 2: 20). But in another sense there is a continuing need for the apostolic faith to be passed on from generation to generation and for Christians constantly to be re-assessing their faith against the touchstone of apostolic doctrine. Thus Paul can charge Timothy, 'what you have heard from me before many witnesses entrust to faithful men who will be able to teach others also' (2 Tim. 2: 2), and Jude can appeal to his readers 'to contend for the faith which was once for all delivered to the saints' (verse 3). Here is the true apostolic succession, entrusting others with the truth of the gospel as displayed in Holy Scripture so that they in their turn will be able to pass it on to others. Here is the true task of the Christian theologian. He is ever to re-examine Christian thinking by the standard of the biblical revelation and to re-express it in terms comprehensible to the age in which he lives. Could not

36

those who are conscious of a specific call to exercise these ministries be truly said to be exercising the gift of apostleship?

A further reason why, in our view, the gift of apostleship cannot be regarded as having been withdrawn with the death of the twelve apostles lies in the second function committed to them, namely, the spreading of the gospel. Christ's command to His disciples to take the gospel into all the world and to every creature is explicitly recorded in the Gospels and in Acts. The church was to be a missionary church reaching out to others with the good news of God's love in Christ and the apostles were to spearhead this missionary outreach. Indeed only when the gospel has been preached throughout the whole world will the church's task be finished, for then the end will come (Mt. 24: 14). Now on each occasion when the Great Commission was given it was given to the eleven apostles and to no others. If they only exercised the gift of apostleship then they only were commissioned to spread the gospel. Indeed, such a conclusion has been held from time to time in the church's history. Yet the continuing spiritual darkness of many areas of the world and the realization that many people have still to hear the gospel for the first time has caused Christians to recognize the continuing need for apostles, those who will go where Christ is not named, there to plant Christian churches. Obviously, the Twelve and Paul were apostles in a special, unrepeatable sense, but cannot the gift of apostleship be discerned in the activities of those who have been used of God in the extension of the church into new areas for the past two thousand years?

Significantly many Christians down the ages have recognized the continuing nature of the gift of apostleship both as regards the function of apostles in preserving purity of doctrine and as regards their function in planting new churches. Thus even Calvin, who states quite clearly that apostles were temporary, in the same breath admits that God 'still occasionally raises them up when the necessity of the time requires' and then asserts that apostles had been necessary in his own day 'to bring back the Church from the revolt of Antichrist'.[3] Similarly outstanding Christian missionaries greatly used of God in carrying the gospel into hitherto unreached areas of the world have earned the title of 'apostle' from their contemporaries and from historians. Thus, for example, Carey has been called 'the Apostle of India', Judson 'the Apostle of Burma', and Aidan is referred to as 'the Apostle of Northumbria'. Sometimes the office of apostle has been specially recognized. Thus the English Baptists of the seventeenth century appointed 'messengers' or 'apostles' with the specific task of pioneering the gospel and establishing new churches, caring for them until they were adequately pastored. The term is not currently in vogue, but are not modern missionaries specifically engaged in planting new churches exercising the gift of apostleship?

Like other spiritual gifts the gift of apostleship is a supernatural gift. Preserving the purity of Christian doctrine requires spiritual qualities and while academic learning is not to be despised, that in itself is insufficient. Paul insisted that his teaching was given 'in words not taught by human wisdom but taught by the Spirit. . . . The unspiritual man does not receive the gifts of the Spirit of God, for they are folly to him, and he is not able to understand them because they are spiritually discerned' (1 Cor. 2: 13, 14). Theologians who see their task as being to make Christian doctrine academically respectable have often ended up diluting or even denying the faith they have claimed to preserve. Contending for the faith once delivered to the saints requires qualities which no amount of learning can give and an ability to teach 'not in plausible words of wisdom, but in demonstration of the Spirit and power, that your faith might not rest in the wisdom of men but in the power of God' (1 Cor. 2: 4, 5).

Similarly, pioneering the gospel in new and sometimes strange and hostile regions requires spiritual qualities which no amount of purely human ability or bravery or patience can give. Indeed nothing is more thrilling to the individual

[3] J. Calvin, *Institutes*, 4, iii. 4.

Christian than to read the stories of God's apostles, ancient and modern, and to see how their whole ministry was accompanied and directed by the evident work of the Spirit of God.

Prophets

Prophecy is an unusual gift in that, while prophets seem to have enjoyed a recognized position in the early church, at the same time the gift of prophecy seems to have been more widely present among church members without such a recognized position. Indeed it would appear from Acts 2: 17, 18 that prophecy is potentially a gift available to all Christians, its presence in the church being one of the marks of the 'Spirit age' which began at Pentecost. In similar vein Paul exhorts all the Corinthian Christians to seek the gift of prophecy in preference to other gifts and advises them, 'You can *all* prophesy one by one' (see 1 Cor. 14: 5, 31). On the other hand, the prophet held a recognized position in the church second only in importance to the apostles. Thus prophets are placed second in two of Paul's lists of offices God has given to the church (see 1 Cor. 12: 28; Eph. 4: 11) and first in a third list (see Rom. 12: 6). Prophets were active in the leadership of the church at Antioch (Acts 13: 1); Agabus, Judas and Silas are also mentioned as being prophets (Acts 11: 28; 15: 32; 21: 10, 11) and Philip had four daughters who prophesied (Acts 21: 9). In this chapter we shall consider the office of prophet and in the next the place of prophecy when it is more widely distributed in the Christian congregation.[4]

Peter's quotation on the day of Pentecost from the Old Testament prophet Joel which we have already cited (see Acts 2: 17, 18) demonstrates that the early Christians saw their prophets as following in the tradition of the Jewish prophets of earlier days. Space forbids an examination here of the rôle and function of the prophet in the history of

[4] See pp. 62ff.

Israel. Voluminous writings exist for the benefit of those wishing to make a special study of the subject and many varying opinions are held by scholars of the highest repute. Suffice to say most scholars are agreed that the Old Testament prophet primarily proclaimed God's Word to the people of his day, and secondarily, in connection with this, often predicted future events. This same combination of proclamation and prediction is found in New Testament prophecy, particularly in the Revelation of John where the two aspects are completely integrated. Other lesser prophets such as Agabus are usually cited when predicting future events (e.g. Acts 11: 28; 21: 10, 11) but undoubtedly they saw their work as including proclamation as well. Indeed a combination of proclamation and prediction can be said to lie at the heart of all Christian teaching. The Christian is commanded to live like Christ and to proclaim Him to others in the light of His predicted return when this present evil world will be destroyed and the Christian's salvation will be complete (see, e.g., 1 Jn. 3: 2, 3).

In 1 Corinthians 14 Paul sets out in detail the rôle of the Christian prophet. First, he says, the prophet speaks to *men* 'for their upbuilding and encouragement and consolation' (1 Cor. 14: 3); secondly 'he who prophesies edifies the *church*' (1 Cor. 14: 4); and thirdly, when Christians prophesy in the church meeting 'and an unbeliever or outsider enters, he is convicted by all, he is called to account by all, the secrets of his heart are disclosed; and so, falling on his face, he will worship God and declare that God is really among you' (1 Cor. 14: 24, 25). With such a wide-ranging ministry to perform for the benefit of the individual Christian, the whole congregation and the unbeliever from outside, is there any wonder that Paul places prophets second only to apostles in his lists of officers in the church?

Having spelled out, then, the rôle of the prophet, we ask how he operates. First, and obviously, the prophet operates by the power of the Holy Spirit. Prophecy is a spiritual gift distributed solely by the Spirit of God. When all prophesy the unbeliever is convicted by all, but he is convicted because the Holy Spirit convinces the world of sin and of righteousness and of judgment (Jn. 16: 8). When gifted Christians prophesy others are strengthened and built up because the Spirit guides His people into all the truth and comforts and strengthens them (see Jn. 14–16). Thus prophecy is not a natural talent which can be taught and developed by human agency alone, and the prophet who forgets the need for God's power in his work and who begins to rely on his own ability will soon cease to function effectively.

Secondly, the prophet operates through speaking; 'he who prophesies *speaks* to men' (1 Cor. 14: 3). By placing prophecy within the context of the church meeting Paul further emphasizes that it is by public speaking that the prophet primarily works. In this connection it is important that the prophet should be in control of himself. Apparently, at Corinth, some of the prophets were prophesying in a frenzy or trance. But this is wrong, says Paul, for 'the spirits of prophets are subject to prophets' (1 Cor. 14: 32). Furthermore, uncritical acceptance must not be given to the prophet's words. The others sitting listening must weigh what is said (see 1 Cor. 14: 29). For although the prophet is the instrument of the Spirit of God he is not infallible, for he is still human and he may err. The discerning congregation must therefore be ready to correct him. The criterion of judgment will be the Word of God as made known through the Old and New Testaments. Paul says, 'If any one thinks that he is a prophet, or spiritual, he should acknowledge that what I am writing to you is a command of the Lord. If any one does not recognize this, he is not recognized' (1 Cor. 14: 37, 38). Thus prophets must accept the authority of the apostolic writings of the New Testament and operate within the limits of their instruction.

In connection with this last point many have found difficulty with Paul's association of 'revelation' with prophecy (see 1 Cor. 14: 26–33). They have supposed that prophets had a particular rôle to play in the early church while the revelation of the New Testament remained incomplete, and they have suggested that, once the New Testament was complete, then there was no further need for prophets and so their gift was withdrawn. This sort of reasoning, however, regards as synonymous God's work of revelation through apostles and through prophets. Undoubtedly this was sometimes the case if God prophesied through an apostle as in the Revelation of John. But there is no need always to regard revelation through apostles now enshrined in the New Testament and revelation through prophets as the same. God is always revealing Himself to His people. He does this primarily and in every age through His Word, but surely He also does this when He applies a passage or a sentence from His Word to a particular Christian's need or situation at a particular time. This is no justification for the dubious method of seeking guidance from the Bible with a pin, or by letting it fall open at random. Scripture must always be studied in its context. Yet most Christians can recall times when different biblical passages met different needs in a vividly personal way. Similarly God reveals Himself through the speaking of His prophets. The prophet is one, as has been seen, who proclaims God's Word and it should always be the prophet's concern that, as he speaks, God will take his words and apply them to the particular needs of those who are listening. In this way his words will be a 'revelation'.

We would argue, therefore, that the prophet is someone who publicly proclaims God's Word to the assembled congregation within the framework of the biblical revelation. In other words he is the expository preacher of Scripture, whether for the strengthening and upbuilding of Christians in a devotional context or for the conversion of unbelievers in an evangelistic setting. Empowered by the Spirit of God for his high and holy task, the prophet seeks the aid of the Spirit in his choice of scriptural passages or themes to expound, and he prays that the Spirit will accompany his words and make them a revelation to those who hear.

Whether or not prophets should be so recognized by name, the continuing need for Christians to exercise the prophetic gift in the modern church should be obvious. The church has always been strong when it has been blessed with those 'mighty in deed and word before God and all the people' (Lk. 24: 19). Perhaps the relative absence of Spirit-filled expository preachers at the present time reflects the spiritual poverty of the modern church. Since it pleases God by the foolishness of preaching to save those who believe (1 Cor. 1: 21) there will be a continuing need for the exercise of the gift of prophecy for as long as God is concerned to build and strengthen His church on earth.

Evangelists

Third in Paul's list in Ephesians 4 of those with special gifts come evangelists. Since both prophets and apostles were responsible for evangelism, the necessity for the inclusion of evangelists as a separate office has been questioned by scholars ancient and modern. Modern writers who reject the Pauline authorship of Ephesians see the whole list of officers as reflecting a post-Pauline era of church government when, with apostles in obvious decline through death and advancing years, evangelists were beginning to be appointed to continue their evangelistic activity. This is really only a modern expression of an older view held by Calvin and others which sees evangelists as apostolic substitutes appointed for the early period of Christian missionary activity only. Their work, according to this view, is now to be incorporated in the office of pastors and teachers for Paul exhorts Timothy to 'do the work of an evangelist' (2 Tim. 4: 5).

Without rejecting the Pauline authorship of Ephesians it must be admitted that Paul's inclusion of 'evangelists' in his list of officers with special gifts is unusual. It is not duplicated in any of the other lists; in them the work of evangelism appears to be covered by other officers. Nonetheless Paul must have included evangelists for a reason and we must seek to discover that reason and ask if evangelists have a continuing place in the church's ministry.

First of all, the view that evangelists appeared as apostolic substitutes only when apostles were already in decline must be rejected as inconsistent with New Testament evidence. Philip is described as an evangelist in Acts 21 : 8 at a time when the apostles were still very much alive and active in the church and some of his evangelistic work is recorded in some detail earlier in Acts (see chapter 8). Secondly, the view that evangelists enjoyed only a temporary ministry in the church's early history must also be rejected on the basis of the meaning of the word itself and on the evidence of later church history.

An evangelist is literally one who preaches the gospel. That this was Philip's special gift is abundantly clear from the description of his work in Acts 8. That this, among other things, was Paul's intention for Timothy is also clear from the passage already cited (2 Tim. 4 : 5). To be sure apostles and prophets also preached the gospel but as part of their wider work, apostles as church planters and prophets as ministers of the Word. Philip was the specialist evangelist. Although in Samaria he preached in a hitherto unevangelized area he did not plant a church there; he waited for the apostles. Neither is there any record of Philip engaging in a ministry wider than evangelism.

While all Christians are required to evangelize in the sense of personal witnessing, church history provides abundant evidence of the fact that God has again and again raised up men with the special gift of communicating the gospel to others and calling for individual repentance and faith. Unlike the apostle or pioneer missionary who plants churches in hitherto unreached areas, such evangelists normally operate within an existing church framework. One outstanding modern example of an evangelist is, of course, Billy Graham; but most readers will probably be able to think of others less well-known, but having the obvious gift of communicating the gospel. Further it should go without saying that the gift of evangelism is a supernatural gift and cannot be acquired by natural means. While it may be accompanied by natural ability in oratory, oratorical prowess alone will never bring men to Christ. This is the work of the Holy Spirit who operates through the words of the evangelist bringing conviction, repentance, faith and regeneration in the heart of the hearer. Because the church is commanded to preach the gospel to every creature, evangelists will always be necessary if the Great Commission is to be fully obeyed. The conferment of this gift should surely be the object of constant prayer by the church's members.

Pastors and teachers

Although some Christians (including Calvin, those who framed the Westminster Confession, and the Puritans of New England) have regarded these as separate offices within the church, the majority of present-day New Testament scholars regard them as one. This is, first, because Paul designates them both by one definite article, and secondly, because every attempt to distinguish between them in practice has proved impracticable. Pastors and teachers are the spiritual overseers of Christian congregations. The Greek word for pastors is the same as for shepherds; hence their task is to 'feed the church of the Lord' by wise counsel and regular instruction. They are to protect the church from division and false teachers and are always to remain subject to the Word of God (see Acts 20: 28–32). They must be of sound moral character and exemplary in the management of their own homes (1 Tim. 3: 1–7).

While the permanence of apostles, prophets and evangelists has been denied by some, pastors and teachers under various names have survived and indeed have remained important in every Christian tradition. On their worth or otherwise has depended the strength of varying Christian communities. Few would deny their need for spiritual abilities above all other qualifications and their place among those supernaturally equipped in the church by the Holy Spirit is obvious. Because of their position of leadership pastors and teachers are particularly prone to the sin of conceit and will always be targets for slander by outsiders (1 Tim. 3: 6, 7). Hence they need specially to guard their contact with God and to rekindle the gift that is within them (2 Tim. 1: 6). For regular Christian instruction, whether through personal contact, pulpit ministry, house-meeting, or any combination of these and other methods, probably does more to strengthen the church than the exercise of any of the other gifts. We should surely expect that, in any appearance of more spectacular gifts within a Christian community, those who exercise such gifts will do so in accordance with the advice and experience and authority of the pastor-teacher, since he is God's gift to the church for this specific purpose.

Other offices in the church

Besides Paul's list in Ephesians 4 of offices in the church for which those who hold the office are supplied with spiritual gifts, other similar offices are suggested in some of the other lists. Thus 'service' in Romans 12: 7 is understood by some commentators to refer to deacons, and 'he who gives aid' in Romans 12: 8 to refer to the officer in charge of the distribution of money to the poor. Similarly 'helpers' and 'administrators' in 1 Corinthians 12: 28 would seem to indicate holders of a recognized office in the church. Indeed the 'helpers' are understood to be deacons by many modern lexicologists, while the 'administrators' are literally those who steer the ship, hence those who govern the church. The list in Ephesians 4 is exclusively concerned with gifts for ministry, and since the early church quickly recognized the need for officers to deal with administration who would free the apostles to continue their spiritual ministry (see Acts 6), it is not surprising that other offices for a similar purpose should be mentioned by Paul. Similar needs have been consistently recognized by the church down through the centuries.

It would seem fruitless to try to determine the detailed differences between the various offices cited above, neither would it seem necessary for churches to try to appoint similar officers with identical names today. The point is that all who assist in the running of the church need spiritual gifts to fulfil their positions adequately. Churches are not business corporations whose main concern is efficiency and profitability. They are part of the body of Christ with spiritual concerns and motives. Hence, while they should not be deliberately inefficient, all those concerned with their ongoing life should be chosen primarily for their spiritual and moral qualities and should seek the enabling of the Holy Spirit to carry out their tasks. When the apostles needed help in the daily distribution to the widows their concern was to choose 'men of good repute, full of the Spirit and of wisdom' (Acts 6: 3). If 'wisdom' refers to natural abilities it is significant that it appears last in the list of qualifications required. Similarly, Paul says that deacons should be men of moral integrity and spiritual understanding before he mentions their proven ability (see 1 Tim. 3: 8–10). In practical terms this means that the church treasurer must, first and foremost, be filled with the Spirit, and only secondly a wizard with figures, and the church caretaker must be more concerned with the spiritual vitality of the church than with fingermarks on polished pews.

The Holy Spirit has provided gifts for those concerned with the upkeep and administration of Christian communities. Happy are those churches where His gifts are sought and applied!

4 GIFTS FOR THE WHOLE CHURCH

From gifts provided for recognized officers in the church we turn now to consider those which are distributed more widely. The basic list is given in 1 Corinthians 12: 8–11, but we shall look also at one or two other passages. Paul makes it abundantly clear that these gifts also are provided by God for the benefit of the church as a whole and are always to be exercised to that end. In the New Testament there is not the distinction which we sometimes make between 'clergy' and 'laity'. All Christians are expected to contribute to the church's well-being and growth. So we find the apostle encouraging all the Corinthian Christians to desire earnestly the spiritual gifts (1 Cor. 14: 1) and recognizing that, when they come together, 'each one has something to contribute from God' (1 Cor. 14: 26).

The utterance of wisdom (*1 Cor. 12: 8*)

Basing their exegesis on the AV translation 'the *word* of wisdom', some writers have concluded that this gift is one of uttering an inspired wise saying in some sort of church meeting which solves a problem or points the way forward in a hitherto intractable situation. Being inspired by the Spirit the word of wisdom is immediately so recognized by the rest of the congregation who then act on the advice supernaturally given. James' settlement of the Council of Jerusalem in Acts 15: 13–21 is evidenced as an instance of this kind. It is reasoned that on the issue of the admission of Gentiles into its ranks the church was facing an intractable problem with various members and parties adopting entrenched positions. Only the Spirit-inspired wisdom of James could have brought the two sides together and prevented a serious and damaging split from occurring. Significantly after James' speech 'it seemed good to the apostles and the elders, with *the whole church*' (Acts 15: 22) to act on his advice. And in the letter of settlement sent to the churches in Antioch, Syria and Cilicia the Council's decision is described as seeming good 'to the Holy Spirit and to us' (Acts 15: 28).

If, however, James' peace formula at the Council of Jerusalem is the sort of thing Scripture means by the utterance of wisdom some problems immediately arise. First, James himself does not appear to have claimed to exercise any specific spiritual gift when suggesting the settlement. He says, '*My* judgment is . . . ' (Acts 15: 19), not 'the Lord's judgment', nor 'the Spirit's judgment'. As already noted James, although not one of the Twelve, was recognized as an apostle and accorded equal status with Peter and John.[1] If he was speaking under the direct inspiration of the Holy Spirit it really is most unusual for him to say '*my* judgment', for the apostles were usually very quick to claim divine authority for their words when they were conscious of this.[2]

Secondly, once it is accepted that *any* individual Christian may give infallible, detailed guidance to a church or other Christian group, the door is opened to all sorts of problems and difficulties. No-one (and this includes Christians) finds it easy to understand the mind of God (see Rom. 11: 33, 34). He does indeed promise to guide His people, but how many readers of this book, for example, can recall times in their Christian lives when, in following a certain

[1] See p. 35.
[2] See, *e.g.*, 1 Corinthians 7: 40 where Paul suggests there could be a difference between his own opinion and teaching inspired by 'the Spirit of God'. *Cf.* also 1 Corinthians 14: 37 with its reference to 'a command of the Lord'.

course of action, they thought they were obeying God's guidance only to discover later how mistaken they were?

The point we are making is that there is no short cut to knowing God's guidance. God guides through day-by-day obedience to His Word in the circumstances in which Christians find themselves, and humility is a constantly-needed grace in this area of Christian living. Often it is only after a series of events that we can see how the sovereign hand of God has guided and protected us. If individual Christians get the idea that through some supernatural gift they can give infallible, detailed guidance to their church or Christian Union, then deep trouble will almost invariably ensue. Indeed, without being uncharitable, it must be recognized that this has been an admitted problem even in those churches which have understood the gift of wisdom as we have outlined it and have sought to exercise it accordingly.

A further problem which may easily arise if the gift of wisdom is seen as the gift of guiding the church in an intractable situation is that, consciously or unconsciously, Christians might find themselves being drawn into some kind of take-over bid for control of their particular church or other fellowship group. In this context the 'word of wisdom' might seek to reverse carefully thought-out policies of the existing leadership. If the 'word of wisdom' is then followed, some degree of leadership will thereafter almost inevitably lie in the one credited with the inspired gift and he may well be able to increase his position of influence with the further passage of time. If the 'inspired word' is not obeyed, then the leadership can be denounced as 'un-spiritual' and a new call to the membership for loyalty and obedience will often result in division. That this has often happened with consequent heartache and disappointment to many involved cannot be denied. Had Christians under-stood more accurately from Scripture the nature of the gift of wisdom such difficulties could well have been avoided.

When confronted with difficult phrases or passages in Scripture it is wise to remember that the key to their understanding often lies in other passages which treat the subject in more detail. Since the subject of wisdom has occupied Paul in the opening chapters of 1 Corinthians could it not be that the gift of the utterance of wisdom is to be understood in the light of his earlier thoughts?

Paul contrasts human wisdom with the wisdom of God in redeeming the world through the death of Christ on the cross. So utterly alien are these two types of wisdom that Paul describes each as being foolish in the eyes of the other. To the wise man of this world it is sheer folly to suggest that men can be saved through the death of a rebel on a cross, yet this is precisely what God has done, 'for the foolishness of God is wiser than men' (1: 25).

Similarly, in proclaiming God's way of salvation, the servant of God must beware of relying on his own ability or on the sorts of argument that appeal to men's standards of wisdom. Instead, in proclaiming Jesus Christ and Him crucified, his human attitude must be one of weakness, much fear and trembling as he seeks for a demonstration of the Spirit and of power, so that his hearers' faith might not rest in the wisdom of men but in the power of God (2: 1–5).

This is because the Christian faith is folly by the standards and criteria of human wisdom. It is wisdom only in the eyes of God. Indeed, because the way of salvation has been decreed by God from eternity it is the only true wisdom. Folly to the rulers of this age, it cannot be taught like human wisdom but needs to be revealed by the Spirit (2: 9, 10). Thus the gospel must be imparted in words not taught by human wisdom but taught by the Spirit, interpreting spiritual truths to those who possess the Spirit.

Might it perhaps be this gift of so proclaiming spiritual truths that those who hear them understand to which Paul is referring in 1 Corinthians 12? If so, it is a gift clearly connected with the gifts of prophecy, evangelism and teaching. All those who proclaim God's word need this gift if their work is to be effective. Yet prophets, evangelists and teachers are not alone in their need of it. They are called to proclaim the Word of God publicly, but all Christians are commanded to make their faith in Christ known, and will need this gift just as much in their personal conversations with unbelievers and in personal counselling of other Christians. If verbal Christian witness is not accompanied by the demonstration of the Spirit and of power then it will be but mere words, unintelligible to those who hear and a consequent object of scorn and derision.

Understood in this way, the gift of the utterance of wisdom is vital for the on-going effectiveness of all Christian witness and teaching. It should not be spurned or dismissed as intended only for the early church, but should be eagerly sought by all who in any way have the opportunity to pass on what they know of Christ to others.

The utterance of knowledge (*1 Cor. 12: 8*)

Some commentators have found difficulty in distinguishing between the utterance of wisdom and this gift which comes second in Paul's list. Undoubtedly there is a close connection between the knowledge of the gospel and the recognition that the gospel is the wisdom of God; but when reference is made to the rest of Scripture a clear distinction between knowledge and wisdom where spiritual things are concerned does emerge.

From time to time in both Old and New Testaments men and women are mentioned who possess knowledge of other men or events which they have not acquired by normal means. Thus Elisha had a reputation for conveying to the king of Israel the words that the king of Syria spoke in the security of his bedchamber (2 Ki. 6: 12), while Peter was able to confront Ananias and Sapphira with the enormity of their deception despite the fact that they had told nobody else of what they had done (Acts 5: 1–11). Jesus, of course, constantly spoke and acted according to His supernatural knowledge of the words and even the thoughts of others.

It could well be that Paul is referring to the ability to

utter knowledge supernaturally acquired when he includes this gift in his list. Undoubtedly some Christians possess this gift and are able, often in personal counselling, to put their finger on a problem which may, quite unconsciously, be eluding the person who is being helped. Certainly ministers engaged in pastoral work need to seek divine help of this kind. Many, indeed, can bear witness to a prompting from God on such occasions which goes far beyond mere shrewdness. But apart from these special instances many Christians may find themselves exercising this gift quite unconsciously when, in personal conversation with someone in deep need, they find themselves saying precisely the right things in the particular situation. Afterwards they are rightly humbled and amazed at the way God used them at the time.

Once it is conceded that a Christian may gain knowledge of another's problem or condition by other than normal means several dangers may arise. First, there could be a failure to distinguish between the gift of the utterance of knowledge and the practice of telepathy and clairvoyance, powers often connected with spiritualism. The gift of knowledge is a gift of the Spirit, owing its source to Him, and only to be exercised at His prompting. It is not given for display or self-aggrandisement but for the benefit of the church, and it must always be exercised with this end in view. Significantly, after Peter's exposure of Ananias and Sapphira 'more than ever believers were added to the Lord, multitudes both of men and women' (Acts 5: 14). Similarly the Christian who possesses this gift must always seek to exercise it in the context of helping others to know the goodness of God.

Secondly, where the gift of knowledge is specifically recognized there will always be the danger of abuse. Great harm can be caused when thoughtless, if well-meaning, Christians who supposedly possess this gift go about purporting to tell others the true nature of their problems and insisting they are right in their diagnoses because they have the Spirit of God. In the authors' view the gift of knowledge like several others in Paul's list is one which should not

53

consciously be sought but only gratefully recognized when it is apparent that it has been granted. Always in its exercise there will be the need for accompanying humility, wisdom and prayer.

Thirdly, those who possess the gift of knowledge will need to guard very carefully against the temptation to pass on their knowledge to others who are not involved. In all personal counselling the need for respecting confidences cannot be overstressed. How much more should supernaturally acquired knowledge of deep-seated personality problems or past sins be protected from the prying minds and gossiping tongues of others. 'To whom much is given, much is required' and this is particularly true where the gift of knowledge is concerned.

Faith (*1 Cor. 12: 9*)

Third in Paul's list of gifts comes faith. This is obviously not saving faith for all Christians possess that, nor is it an understanding of the body of teaching sometimes called 'the faith'. The gift of faith is the outstanding faith given to some Christians enabling them to rely on God in a special way for the accomplishment of some specific task, or for the provision for their daily needs, or for some special demonstration of His nature and power. Faith which is given in this way is the faith which dares, the faith which moves mountains, the faith which expects great things from God and which, in consequence, attempts great things for God. This gift of faith has thus lain behind many missionary endeavours and has resulted in men and women hazarding their lives for the gospel. This gift led George Müller to give away all he had and establish an orphanage without any visible means of financial support in order to demonstrate that God cared and would provide for His children. Scriptural examples of many who exercised this gift are listed in Hebrews 11 in order to encourage others to put their whole trust in God in their daily lives. Through the gift of faith the church marches on and the church's enemies are defeated and often made to look foolish in the eyes of their contemporaries. Christian biography is rich in astonishing and moving examples of what can happen when believers are challenged to believe. The continuing need for the exercise of the gift of faith should be obvious to all and the church should always be grateful when it is granted. Through it the church is built up and strengthened and extended.

Gifts of healing (1 Cor. 12: 9)

We come now to what is, perhaps, the first real area of controversy in this book. Undoubtedly the subject of miraculous healing has sometimes aroused Bible-believing Christians to degrees of heat and argument out of all proportion to the place the subject has in the Bible as a whole. In the practice or denial of the validity of this gift, too, extreme positions have been adopted by Christians holding varying viewpoints with unbecoming accusations being made on the one hand and wild and extravagant claims being advanced on the other. Thus some Christians have denounced the work of those who have exercised these gifts as illusory or even satanically inspired. Other Christians have claimed to have healed miraculously in the name of Christ when patently they have not done so. Yet others have concluded that biblical commands to heal in the name of Christ have made the work of doctors and the use of medicines in the cure of diseases unnecessary and obsolete. Our aim in what follows is not to add fuel to the flames but to set out what in our view is biblical teaching on this difficult and often perplexing subject.

That the Bible contains examples of supernatural healing cannot be denied except at the cost of denying the veracity of the Bible itself. In both Old and New Testaments miracles of healing, like other miracles, occur at times when God is particularly active on behalf of His people. We find them taking place, for example, during the Exodus and the wilderness wanderings of the Israelites. They recur during the days of Elijah and Elisha when God was recalling His erring people from their faithless ways. They are a particular feature of the ministry of Jesus and they are very closely, if not inseparably, connected with the evangelistic work of the early church. Jesus' command to His disciples to heal the sick (Mt. 10: 8), His assertion that the works He did His disciples would do also because He was going to the Father (Jn. 14: 12), the inclusion of gifts of healing in Paul's list of gifts in 1 Corinthians 12 and James' instructions for the treatment of the sick (Jas. 5: 13–16) all point to the conclusion that miraculous healing has a place in the ministry of the church. Admittedly the gift of healing has sometimes been abused and has sometimes fallen into disuse; but these are no arguments against it.

Something needs to be said, however, about the teaching of the New Testament on the way gifts of healing are to be exercised. First, miraculous healing must always be viewed against the background of the teaching of the whole of Scripture on the subjects of suffering, disease and death. This is far too large a subject to receive detailed treatment here. Clearly, however, Scripture teaches that suffering, sickness and death are part of man's condition as a result of the fall and will pass away only when God makes His new heaven and new earth (see Rev. 21: 4). In this life none can guarantee exemption or protection from them and the servants of God, like Job, are sometimes those most sorely afflicted. Thus, miraculous healing provides no universal panacea for dealing with sickness. Both Jesus and the apostles must have passed by many who were ill without healing them. Paul prayed three times for deliverance from a thorn in the flesh, each time without success (2 Cor. 12: 8, 9). Epaphroditus fell ill and was near to death, and although he recovered through the mercy of God there does not seem to be any suggestion that he was miraculously healed (Phil. 2: 25–30). In this connection it must be stressed that Scripture nowhere forbids the use of normal means in the treatment of sickness and disease. Thus Timothy is encouraged to use a little wine for the sake of his stomach and his frequent ailments (1 Tim. 5: 23), while Luke, the beloved physician (Col. 4: 14), holds an honoured place in the New Testament and appears to travel with Paul as though he were his personal doctor.

Secondly, miraculous healing in Scripture is always associated with the revelation of the character of God. 'Miracles do not appear on the pages of Scripture, vagrantly, here, there and elsewhere indifferently, without assignable reason,' says B. B. Warfield. 'They belong to revelation periods.'[3] Supernatural healing in both Old and New Testaments demonstrates the concern of God with sickness and suffering and the compassion of God active in its cure and alleviation. In the Old Testament the gift of healing when exercised by the prophet is seen to be in vindication of his God-appointed ministry, while in the New Testament supernatural healing bears witness to the power of the risen Christ through whom God is now made known to men and women. Not surprisingly, therefore, it is often associated with evangelism, being exercised to prove that Christ is alive and concerned with the redemption of the whole man.

The importance of the recognition of this cannot be overstressed when miraculous healing is sought in the modern church. The motive of those who would heal, and in many cases of those who would be healed, must be the glorifying of God and the uplifting of Christ, for only in this context should supernatural healing be even prayed for.

While it is obvious from what Paul says about the distribution of gifts that some Christians will be recognized as possessing the gifts of healing (the word is plural), great care must be taken to avoid personal fame or popularity on that account. Although because of their powers of healing the apostles on occasion seem to have become the objects of mass hysteria (see, e.g., Acts 5: 15; 19: 11), there is never any suggestion that they encouraged such behaviour nor

[3] B. B. Warfield, *Miracles: Yesterday and Today, True and False* (Eerdmans, 1953).

that it lasted for any great length of time. Modern Christians called by God to exercise the gifts of healing may similarly find themselves resisting undue adulation on the part of others (and even exploitation) and will constantly need to ask if the exercise of their gift is always bringing home the reality of the power of Christ to others. Christ's oft-repeated injunction to silence on the part of those who had been healed seems relevant in this connection. In an age when the mass media are constantly on the lookout for drama and sensation sometimes the less said about a miraculous healing the better lest the wrong impression is created.

Thirdly, the close connection often found in Scripture between faith and miraculous healing must be recognized. Jesus Himself often healed in response to faith (see Lk. 7: 1–10; Mk. 2: 5) or else He demanded faith before healing (see Mk. 9: 23). Similarly it was faith in the name of Jesus which gave the cripple at the Beautiful Gate of the Temple his perfect health (Acts 3: 16). Again, it was when Paul saw that the cripple at Lystra had faith to be made well that he commanded him to stand on his feet (Acts 14: 9, 10), while James says, 'the prayer of faith will save the sick man' (Jas. 5: 15). This connection, it must be admitted, has often created practical problems when divine healing has been sought. Some Christians have sadly made a very crude connection between faith and God's ability to heal, making the latter depend on the degree of the former. Thus they have caused unnecessary heartache and suffering in those who have sought healing for themselves or others, and have not found it, by attributing the failure to the seekers' lack of faith. Yet this is a quite false and unscriptural line of reasoning. It is the power of God and the presence of faith which bring healing and not the pressure of faith on the reluctance of God. Jesus spoke of faith small as a grain of mustard seed (Mt. 17: 20; Lk. 17: 6) as being all that is necessary for the accomplishment of God's purposes, and when the prayer of faith does not receive the expected answer this must not be attributed to the believer's lack of faith but left with the loving purpose of God.

Fourthly, Scripture also makes a frequent connection between confession and forgiveness of sin and miraculous healing. Thus Miriam was cured of leprosy only after Aaron admitted that he and she had sinned (see Nu. 12, particularly verse 11); Christ healed the paralytic borne by four only after forgiving his sins (see Mk. 2: 1–12); and in his instructions for the treatment of the sick James associates forgiveness of sins with healing and advises, 'therefore confess your sins to one another . . . that you may be healed' (Jas. 5: 15, 16). In view of modern understanding of the psychosomatic nature of many illnesses and the not infrequent connection between physical illness and deep-seated guilt feelings, all this is particularly significant and must always be remembered by those who are called to exercise the gifts of healing.

Scripture gives no encouragement to those who brashly go around indiscriminately laying hands on all and sundry, claiming to heal in the name of Jesus. It is God who heals as and when He pleases. Sometimes He may respond to the prayers of His people without the use of any 'third party'. But at other times the Holy Spirit may raise up someone to be His special instrument in this ministry to His people. Those who are called to exercise this gift undoubtedly need a deep and sympathetic understanding of human nature and a willingness to proclaim fearlessly the Christ who comes to man in his distress and transforms his whole personality, meeting his physical, mental, intellectual and spiritual needs. Sometimes the acceptance of Christ's forgiveness and salvation will result in the healing of some prolonged and nagging illness, or maybe in release from a deep-seated personality problem. Always Christ's salvation, when truly accepted, will produce wholeness of character where there was failure before. Sometimes healing may be instantaneous and dramatic, perhaps associated with the laying-on of hands or the anointing with oil in the name of the Lord. At other times healing may follow gradually after much prayer and dedication. On other occasions suffering may be borne for a lifetime for no apparent reason. Always the Christian's view of healing will be modified by the Christian's view of death. Death, when it comes, whether by martyrdom, sickness, accident or old age, is *always* in the providence of God and *always* means to be with Christ which is far better (Phil. 2: 23).

Working of miracles (*1 Cor. 12: 10*)

Obviously closely associated with gifts of healing is the power to perform miracles in the name of the Lord. Those recorded in Scripture are comparatively rare, being particularly associated, as has been already noted, with the lives of Moses, Elijah and Elisha and our Lord. In the early church the deliverance of the apostles from prison (Acts 5: 19; 12: 1–11) and Paul's blinding of the false prophet Bar-Jesus at the residence of Sergius Paulus (Acts 13: 4–12) are examples of miracles other than miracles of healing.

Throughout the Bible miracles always vindicate the name of God or protect and deliver His people from some particular danger, either temporary or prolonged, and we may infer that such will be the results of true miracles today. Prayer will be closely associated with their performance and they will be seen as God's way of answering that prayer. Christians need not be disturbed that many miracles, ancient and modern, bear some natural explanation. There is no reason why God should not use natural means in the execution of His will. The miraculous nature of an event may be seen in its association with answered prayer and in its order and timing rather than in any breaking of natural laws. In fact the whole tension between the miraculous and the natural, it seems to us, is a product of modern thinking of a certain kind. It springs from the nineteenth- and twentieth-century conflict between religion and dogmatic, atheistic science. The Christian is affected by this. But the Bible view of the universe is never that of a mechanistic, self-contained system which 'runs on its own'. There is no word for 'Nature' in Hebrew, and no word for 'miracle' as popularly understood today. The whole universe is seen as created, sustained and providentially governed by God who 'makes the grass to grow', 'visits the earth and waters it' and 'accomplishes all things according to the counsel of his own will'. Thus it seems that, in biblical thinking, the difference between a 'natural event' and a 'miracle' is not that in the first God lets things take their own course and in the second God interferes. Rather, in the 'natural event' God is at work providentially in ways unremarked because they are not unusual, whilst in the 'miracle' God is at work so strikingly that attention is drawn, amazement expressed, and truth about His love or His judgment dramatically underlined. Hence the various Hebrew and Greek words used in Scripture to describe the miraculous – sign, token, portent, wonder, mighty deed, power, *etc.* – really describe the effect on those who witness it. Perhaps, therefore, the question 'Does God perform miracles today?' should be rephrased, to read: 'May we pray and act today in the belief that God is always at work, and that He will act in our situations in whatever way He chooses?' To that question there can surely be but one answer.

Strangely, however, many Christians seem frightened of the miraculous in the biblical sense of the word, and hesitant to claim the gift of the working of miracles in their personal lives and in the witness of their churches. Yet Jesus who Himself was 'attested . . . by God with mighty works and wonders and signs which God did through him' (Acts 2: 22) promised that 'he who believes in me will also do the works that I do; and greater works than these will he do, because I go to the Father' (Jn. 14: 12). Surely this promise must embrace the fact that, as His work was miraculous, so should be the work of His followers. The life of the early church as recorded in the Acts of the Apostles would seem to confirm the point. No-one who takes that story seriously can deny that that church lived and grew in the atmosphere of the supernatural and, more importantly, its members considered it normal that this should be so. Linked with their prayers for boldness in their preaching went a confident expectation that God would stretch out His hand to heal and that signs and wonders would be performed through the name of His holy servant Jesus (Acts 4: 30).

If it should be asked how the works of Jesus' followers can be greater than those of Jesus Himself perhaps the answer lies in the fact that they are more widespread. During His earthly ministry Jesus could work only in one place at a time. After the Ascension and Pentecost ('*because I go to the Father*') He can work by the Holy Spirit wherever His people are serving Him. Or perhaps the answer lies in the fact that through the work of evangelism God works His mightiest miracle, the regeneration of men and women dead in trespasses and sins.

Despite many Christians' hesitancy where the working of miracles is concerned it is surely significant that Christians under persecution and Christians pioneering the gospel under dangerous conditions seem more aware of this gift than many of their contemporaries, and the accounts of their lives often contain events which can only be understood as miraculous. Perhaps as the church in Western countries, where it has long enjoyed freedom and privilege, comes under increasing pressure and hostility, Christians in these lands may once again see more of the mighty works of God vindicating the gospel and working powerfully in the lives of men and women to bring them to Christ and His kingdom.

Prophecy (*1 Cor. 12: 10*)

Next in Paul's list of gifts distributed throughout the church comes prophecy. We have already given detailed consideration to this gift in the previous chapter within the specific context of the recognized office of prophet and all that we said there applies here. But we give further consideration to it here because it would seem that at Corinth the gift of prophecy was not confined to recognized prophets but was more widely distributed in the church. Furthermore, when exercised by the many at Corinth, prophecy seems to have had a slightly different character than when it was exercised by the recognized prophet.

We suggested earlier that the prophet is the expository preacher of God's Word. He speaks to men for their upbuilding and encouragement and consolation, to the church for its edification, and to the unbeliever for his conversion. Whereas all prophecy at Corinth must have been of this nature, for these conclusions about it were drawn from 1 Corinthians 14, the prophecy of which we now speak can hardly have been the kind of prepared discourse understood as expository preaching by modern readers. When Paul says, 'you can all prophesy one by one' (1 Cor. 14: 31) he can hardly have been thinking of a succession of thirty-minute sermons! Indeed his words are set in the context of a meeting for informal worship when each member present contributes 'a hymn, a lesson, a revelation, a tongue or an interpretation . . . so that all may learn and all be encouraged' (verses 26, 31). The terms 'revelation' and 'prophecy' are used synonymously (see verses 29-32) and this has led some writers to conclude that prophecy is a brief, unprepared statement given under the direct inspiration of the Holy Spirit. It has been claimed that this and this alone is what the New Testament understands by prophecy and meetings have been arranged where this gift has been sought and exercised.

With this conclusion we would not entirely disagree so long as certain safeguards are observed and so long as Christians remain aware of the whole of New Testament teaching on the gift of prophecy as outlined earlier. Increasing numbers of Christians are finding great value in meeting together in an informal setting for the kind of worship Paul outlines. They seek the Spirit's direction as one or another leads in the singing of a hymn, the reading of a passage from the Bible, or the giving of a prophecy, that is, the speaking of a sentence or a series of sentences which come into the mind and are then passed on to the assembled gathering. Christians do not need to be accomplished preachers to exercise the gift of prophecy in this way and thus to benefit the whole church.

While prophecy is 'revelation', that is, while it makes the mind or will of God clear, it must never be exalted to the level of biblical revelation. This is a point we made earlier but it bears repetition in the present context. A few impromptu sentences in an informal meeting, however relevant and meaningful they may be to some or all the people there, can never take the place of the Word of God in the life of the church or the individual Christian. Prophecy may illuminate the meaning of the Scriptures; it can never replace them.

A further safeguard necessary where informal prophecy is exercised is to avoid expecting that the Holy Spirit will spell out everything for us in great detail. Any attempt to give highly specific instructions to the group, or to individuals in it, under the guise of prophecy should be strenuously discouraged by the leaders of the meeting because of problems which will almost invariably arise as a result. Young people's groups need to be particularly careful here and to avoid all suggestions of others' vocations, careers, future life-partners and the like. Nor can anything but harm be done if responsible committees of Christians put the supposed value of such spontaneous utterances or ideas in some kind of opposition to the need for planning programmes, booking speakers, and making sensible provision for the future.

In our experience, while prophecies have sometimes spoken very directly to individuals' needs, the Christians giving the prophecies have always been personally unaware of these needs, and each prophecy has always been couched in general terms perfectly acceptable to the whole gathering. Only later has the specific usefulness of the prophecy been realized when the Christian particularly spoken to has testified to its helpfulness, thereby at the same time confirming that the Holy Spirit was the prophecy's Author.

Just as the preaching of the recognized prophet will consist largely in the exposition of Scripture, so the content of the informal prophecy will be scriptural and may consist of little more than scriptural phrases and ideas. Anything more than this, or anything at variance with scriptural principles and teaching, should be treated with great reserve and suspicion. We are instructed to 'weigh what is said' (1 Cor. 14: 29) and that must mean checking it against the Word of God.

Yet another safeguard necessary in meetings where informal prophecy may occur will lie in the preservation of decency and order. Paul makes much of this, forbidding simultaneous prophesying by more than one person at a time (1 Cor. 14: 29–31) and forbidding ecstatic and uncontrolled prophesying. Sometimes extreme emotionalism has characterized prophesying in modern times, but 'the spirits of the prophets are subject to the prophets' (1 Cor. 14: 32), so obviously such emotionalism is not only unnecessary but also forbidden by the New Testament.

It is impossible to consider informal prophecy in the context of 1 Corinthians 14 without at the same time giving some consideration to the kind of worship outlined in verse 26 of which it is a part. Is Paul advocating completely unplanned and impromptu worship here for all Christians, and hence, by inference, condemning the more formal and liturgical forms of worship with which we are all so familiar? Some would answer in the affirmative and would use this verse to justify their particular form of worship where different members of the congregation contribute to the service in an unplanned way. Others, on the other hand, would reason that Paul is here merely reflecting the kind of worship which undoubtedly existed in the early church but which later, quite rightly, gave way to more stylized and liturgical forms.

Once again we are in an area of controversy with a rich scholarly literature available to those who wish to pursue it. Perhaps the answer to the problem lies, not in an 'either/or' judgment on informal or liturgical worship, but in a 'both/ and' solution. That the earliest Christians continued worshipping for a time in the Temple suggests that they were not averse to liturgical worship. Similarly their Jewish heritage makes it virtually certain that they would continue to use set forms of worship, albeit with a Christian content, when their connection with the Temple was severed. That Paul could write as he did to the Corinthians also shows that New Testament Christians were no strangers to more informal worship of the type already outlined.

Thus what is needed in the church is not just liturgical nor just informal worship, but both. Indeed this is recognized in many churches. At certain times the church meets for a service with a recognized form and order. At other times, perhaps not even on church premises but in members' homes, the church meets to pray informally and perhaps to exercise appropriate spiritual gifts as well. Some bodies have experimented with services where liturgical praying and singing is combined with the exercise of the *charismata* and many present have testified to the meaningful and beneficial nature of these services. As long as general scriptural principles are observed there is obviously room for rich variety where worship is concerned, and all Christians would do well to learn from the traditions and experience of others in this field, rather than restrict their worship to what is usual and familiar to themselves.

The ability to distinguish between spirits (*1 Cor. 12: 10*)

Like the gift of prophecy, this is another spiritual gift which is potentially available to all Christians, for the apostle John says to all his readers, 'Do not believe every spirit, but test the spirits to see whether they are of God' (1 Jn. 4: 1). In practice, however, its exercise will probably be limited to a fairly small number of Christians who will use the gift reluctantly when occasion demands.

Many non-Christians, and some Christians as well, would deny the validity of this gift altogether. They would base their conclusions on the reasoning that all mention of evil spirits and demon possession in the Bible reflects the thinking of a period in human history when all mental disorders were attributed to the work of personal spiritual forces. Not only has modern psychological and psychiatric understanding demonstrated, they would say, the falseness of such view but modern intelligent people need no longer believe in a personal devil either.

While not denying the necessity of distinguishing between mental disorders and spiritual possession, this is a view we cannot share for a number of reasons. First, denial of the reality of Satan and other evil personal beings ultimately compromises the integrity of Scripture. From Genesis to Revelation the biblical writers portray evil forces in a personal way and record Christ as having accomplished ultimate victory over them at the cross. Similarly the Bible ends with a vivid description of the final destruction of Satan (Rev. 20) and the triumph of Christ (Rev. 21, 22). If Satan as a personal evil being does not exist then in the final analysis many scriptural passages become meaningless.

Secondly, denial of the reality of evil spirits has been consistently rendered invalid by many missionary reports over a long period of time. While for some hundreds of years Western nations may have been largely free from the results of direct demon possession, such has not been the case in many communities overseas where worship of spirits with attendant problems of possession has continued to flourish. There the ability to distinguish between spirits has been a continuing necessary spiritual gift, often granted more frequently to local Christians than to the missionary from abroad.

Thirdly, the resurgence in the West within the past ten years of many different kinds of occult practices, including Satanism, has cast renewed doubt on the confident conclusions of so-called scientific rationalists who have denied the reality of personal spiritual beings. Increasing numbers of

Christians from many different traditions have found themselves confronted with men and women possessed of the devil and have found they have needed the ability to distinguish between spirits and to cast them out in the name of Christ. In the early church this gift became regularized into the office of exorcist. A recent Church of England report has recommended the appointment of exorcists once more in areas where problems arising from occult behaviour are particularly prevalent.

We would suggest, therefore, that the ability to distinguish between spirits is a valid spiritual gift like all the others listed in the New Testament, and that it has particular relevance to the present situation. Having said this, however, certain words of caution must be offered, for this gift, like so many others, has been misunderstood and abused by Christians from time to time.

First, a distinction must always be drawn between direct demon possession and spiritual attacks which come to all Christians in the form of temptation. Some Christians have made the mistake of diagnosing possession as the cause of every kind of Christian failure. This is quite wrong. Temptation to sin is a normal experience in every human life, Christian or otherwise. Most Christians will admit to finding certain kinds of temptation more attractive than others and will suffer from what are called 'besetting sins'. From time to time all Christians sin (see 1 Jn. 1 : 8), but this does not mean, even if they have persistent problems with particular sins, that they are possessed. There seems to be a connection between possession and dabbling in the various kinds of occult behaviour and, as this is expressly forbidden on several occasions in the Bible (see, *e.g.*, Lv. 19: 26, 31; Dt. 18: 9–14), the Christian who knowingly breaks God's law on this point may be more prone to direct satanic attack as a result than the ignorant non-Christian.

Secondly, as has been suggested already, a further distinction must also be made between mental illness and spirit possession. While the two may occur simultaneously, and while possession may cause or worsen mental illness, there is no necessary connection between them. This must be remembered particularly when help is offered to Christians who are mentally ill. Just as Christians are prone to physical illness, so they may fall victim to mental illness. Nothing can be more harmful to those who are so distressed than to be told they are possessed of the devil and for an instantaneous cure to be attempted by exorcism. Even when possession is accompanied by mental illness (and this will not always be the case) it will be evidenced not so much in the symptoms of mental illness as in opposition to the gospel and the servants of God. Reading of Christ's victory over spirits to one who is possessed often produces a reaction which will confirm the presence of one or more evil spirits. Then and only then should the spirits be cast out in the name of Christ.

Thirdly, the New Testament would seem to suggest that the ability to distinguish between spirits should be sought only when confrontation is made with those who may be possessed. Significantly, in all the ministry of Paul, we read only once of his casting out an evil spirit, and this he did apparently reluctantly after being pestered for many days by the girl who was possessed (Acts 16: 16–18). Many Christians who have similarly been forced by circumstances into exorcism have told of the mental, physical and emotional exhaustion which they have suffered as a result. While they have rejoiced in the victory which has been accomplished in the name of Christ they nonetheless speak of shrinking from further direct confrontation with the Evil One because of its effects. How different is this from the activities of some Christians who lightheartedly run around looking for spirits to cast out! Such do not seem to know the power of the forces with which they are playing nor the potential harm they may be causing by their tactless behaviour.

There *is* release in the name of Christ for those who are possessed. There *is* victory in the name of Christ for Christians who are confronted with those who are possessed and who, perhaps in the circumstances of the moment, have no-

69

one to whom they can turn for help. But this gift, perhaps more than many of the others, needs wisdom and care and discernment in its exercise, and such can come only from the Spirit of God Himself.

It may well be that the 'discerning of spirits' also refers to a less dramatic but more common situation. When teaching which purports to be from God is presented to our attention, we must remember that there is a 'spirit of error' as well as the Spirit of truth. Religious teachers can be demonically deceived, misled by their own pride, and deceivers of their hearers. 1 John 4: 1–6 gives this warning. The enemy of God has ruined the lives of many, both through the activities of so-called 'fringe-cults' (Mormons, Jehovah's Witnesses, *etc.*) and through the speculations of leading 'theologians' who have destroyed the faith and confused the minds of their readers. In the first case there is always some occult experience or special revelation in the background. In the second case there is sadly often an intellectual arrogance which feels free to dethrone God and His Word, and which closely resembles the pride which caused Satan to fall.

The Christian needs to be discerning when he is confronted by new religious teachers. Often he will find within himself an uneasiness, an instinctive shrinking, which gives him time to weigh words carefully and to discern their hidden import. The apostle John tells us that when we are confronted by the claims of an alleged teacher, our response should be spiritual and mental, not emotional. The emotional reaction might be to say, 'How enthusiastic he is! How convinced he seems! How eagerly he assures me of his love! How impressively his words pour out!' The spiritual approach is to ask a question: 'Has Christ come in the flesh?' In other words, apostolic doctrine, the pre-existence of Christ, the reality of His incarnation, the completeness of His atonement – spiritual truth spiritually taught and relevantly applied – this is the touchstone for those who need to 'discern the spirits'.

Various kinds of tongues and the interpretation of tongues (*1 Cor. 12: 10*)

Because of their obvious close connection we consider these two gifts together, perhaps the most controversial of all the spiritual gifts listed in the New Testament. Until very recently rejection or acceptance of the validity of these gifts has bitterly divided evangelical Christians, and although we hope a new spirit of tolerance is abroad today many of the old suspicions and prejudices remain. Most of the objections in modern times to speaking with tongues spring from the strangeness of the phenomenon, misunderstanding about its nature, confusion about its purpose, or reaction against the exaggerated importance attached to it by some Christians. Yet the gift is not only listed by Paul in 1 Corinthians but given considerable treatment in the form of instructions about its exercise. In the Acts of the Apostles mention is made of the occurrence of the gift at several crucial points in the history of the early church. Thus, if Christians are to be faithful to the New Testament, they cannot ignore the existence of speaking with tongues and, as with all the other gifts, must seek to understand it and to regulate its exercise according to New Testament teaching.

The first thing which is apparent from Paul's description of the gift in 1 Corinthians is that speaking in tongues is speaking in languages. The languages may be languages of men or they may be languages of angels (13: 1) but they are languages all the same. It is important to establish this point, for many think that the utterances of those who speak in tongues are gibberish resulting from their highly charged emotional state or from a deliberate attempt by the use of gibberish to demonstrate the gift. Unfortunately, support has been given to this view from two sources. Some enthusiasts for tongues-speaking have accepted emotional gibberish as a true manifestation of the gift, and some translators of and commentators on the New Testament have used such phrases as 'ecstatic utterance' and 'tongues of ecstasy' to describe the gift. Such phrases do not reflect the true sense of the original Greek and seem to indicate considerable confusion about the nature of the gift.

From the language used in the New Testament it is reasonable to conclude that the sound of speaking in tongues is not the sound of ecstatic gibberish but is basically the same as the sound of someone speaking another language, in which sentences, words and syntax will be clearly audible to the careful listener and their basic structure repeated when a translation or 'interpretation' is given. A highly charged emotional atmosphere will not be necessary for the exercise of the gift, and the speaker will remain in full control of his faculties while speaking. Just as a Christian who is praying in his native language may stop praying if external circumstances make it inconvenient or improper for him to continue, so one who is speaking in tongues will similarly be able to cease if necessary. Uncontrolled or uncontrollable speaking with tongues is not the phenomenon described in the New Testament.

Secondly, Paul describes the gift of tongues as a means of addressing God: 'one who speaks in a tongue speaks not to men but to God' (14: 2). In other words speaking with tongues is a form of prayer, and Paul goes on to make it clear that it is a form of prayer directly inspired by the Holy Spirit: 'no one understands him, but he utters mysteries in the Spirit' (14: 2). The same thought recurs later in verse 14 of the same chapter: 'If I pray in a tongue, my spirit prays but my mind is unfruitful.' It does not matter whether the RSV translation is read here or the NEB translation, 'the Spirit in me prays', for true spiritual prayer always comes at the prompting of the Holy Spirit.

There would appear to be a real connection between Paul's words here and his teaching on the work of the Holy Spirit in Romans 8: 26 where he writes, 'the Spirit helps us in our weakness; for we do not know how to pray as we ought, but the Spirit himself intercedes for us with sighs too deep for words'. While this verse does not mean that prayer in tongues is the only form of Spirit-prompted prayer, it would seem to suggest that praying in incomprehensible words is one form which Spirit-directed prayer can take. Christians must never fall into the trap of thinking that praying in tongues removes the need for praying in one's native tongue, for Paul says in 1 Corinthians 14: 15, 'I will pray with the spirit and I will pray with the mind also,' and the Christian can be confident that the Holy Spirit will prompt both kinds of prayer. Indeed many Christians have found such a combination of praying in tongues and praying normally particularly helpful, and in unusually difficult situations they have testified to the way in which praying in tongues has helped them to pray more intelligently and fervently in their native language.

Closely connected with praying in the spirit in 1 Corinthians 14 are 'singing with the spirit' and 'blessing with the spirit' (verses 15, 16) and here a further comparison can be made with Ephesians 5 where Paul lists 'addressing one another in . . . spiritual songs' as distinct from 'psalms and hymns' as one of the results of being 'filled with the Spirit' (verses 18, 19). Again, Paul is not suggesting that all Spirit-filled Christians should sing in tongues, but he would appear to be saying that such singing (for this is what we interpret 'spiritual songs' as being) is one quite natural and normal way in which a Christian might address God and his fellow-believers.

Thirdly, Paul demonstrates that speaking with tongues has both private and public use and value. This is obvious from his assertion in 1 Corinthians 14: 18 that he speaks in tongues more than the Corinthians themselves, yet in church he would rather speak five words with his mind, to instruct others, than ten thousand words in a tongue. Thus the private exercise of tongues is preferable to its public exercise. 'He who speaks in a tongue edifies himself' (14: 4), and herein lies the main value of tongues to the individual believer. Along with prayer in his native language, along with Bible study, along with corporate worship and participation in the Lord's Supper, along with the joy of witnessing to others, speaking in tongues builds him up. It does not replace nor is it a substitute for any of these other activities but is to be used alongside them. As previously noticed, Paul says, 'I will pray with the spirit and I will pray with the mind also' (14: 15).

Because prayer in tongues is incomprehensible to those who hear, Paul forbids its use in public unless it is accompanied by interpretation. When interpretation is given, then the church is edified (14: 5) and the gift would then appear to be equal in value with prophecy (see 14: 1–5). Interpretation of tongues may come through the one who has spoken in tongues (for Paul says in 14: 13, 'he who speaks in a tongue should pray for the power to interpret'), or it may come through another member of the group with the known gift of interpretation (*cf.* 12: 10, 30; 14: 27, 28). Indeed the latter might seem to be the more normal course, for Paul says that if there is no-one to interpret those who would speak in tongues should keep silence in church and speak to themselves and to God (see 14: 28).

Like all the other gifts, the abilities to speak in tongues and to interpret speaking in tongues are supernatural endowments of the Holy Spirit. The interpreter does not normally naturally understand the language of the tongue (although when this occasionally happens it is a welcome confirmation of the reality of the gift), but is enabled to understand and interpret the language by the direct work of the Holy Spirit. It is fair to ask how such interpretation is given. Many Christians have discovered they possess this gift when, after a prayer in a tongue in a meeting they have felt impelled to speak a sentence in English which has come into their minds. As they have spoken this sentence another sentence has come into their minds and so on until the prayer has been fully interpreted. Without wishing to be dogmatic it would seem that this is the normal way in which interpretations are given.

By limiting speaking in tongues to two or three different people in any one meeting (14: 27) Paul guards against the situation of allowing this gift to dominate a gathering. By insisting on interpretation in a meeting Paul ensures that tongues shall be used for edification. 'Let all things be done for edification,' he says (14: 26). By defining the purpose of tongues as a means of addressing God, Paul sets the gift in the context of worship as opposed to, say, an enjoyable thrill, or a means of showing off to others.

This function of tongues as a means of worship finds confirmation elsewhere in the New Testament. Thus on the day of Pentecost the Jewish pilgrims in Jerusalem heard the disciples telling in their own tongues '*the mighty works of God*' (Acts 2: 11). Thus at Caesarea the Jewish believers who had accompanied Peter to the home of Cornelius were amazed when the Holy Spirit was poured out on the Gentiles, 'for they heard them speaking in tongues *and extolling God*' (Acts 10: 46). Thus at Ephesus the dozen believers in John's baptism who were baptized into the name of the Lord Jesus 'spoke with tongues *and prophesied*' (Acts 19: 6). While undoubtedly speaking with tongues occurred on each of these three occasions to confirm that the Holy Spirit had been given, it is still significant that the New Testament records that the phenomenon was linked with the glorifying of God and the encouraging of others in accordance with the principles laid down in 1 Corinthians.

Many twentieth-century Christians have reacted violently against speaking with tongues for a variety of reasons. Some have been offended by the demands of some teachers on the subject that all Christians should speak in tongues in order to demonstrate that they have been filled with the Holy Spirit. This is a serious objection and is dealt with at length in the central portion of this book.[4]

Quite apart from this objection, however, other Christians have forbidden the exercise of tongues in their fellowships on the basis of Paul's assertion in 1 Corinthians 13: 8 that tongues will cease. Consideration of this objection as far as gifts in general are concerned has already been made earlier in the book[5] and the reasoning adopted there remains valid where specific objection is made to speaking with

[4] See pp. 101ff., 133ff.
[5] See pp. 26ff.

tongues. To forbid the exercise of this gift on the basis of 1 Corinthians 13: 8 is to lift this verse completely out of its context. More impressive, and completely in context, are Paul's words in 1 Corinthians 14: 5 and 39, 'Now I want you all to speak in tongues' and 'do not forbid speaking in tongues'.

The fact that outside the special incidents in Acts the gift of tongues is mentioned only in the church at Corinth has led some to suppose that this church alone had any regular exercise of the gift. It is suggested that Paul was embarrassed by the unusual phenomenon and came as near as he could to banning it without actually doing so. It is also pointed out that the Corinthian church was in a notoriously bad condition spiritually so that the exercise of tongues there, of all places, is no commendation of the gift.

This argument takes its propounders too far, however, for it casts doubt on the integrity and authority of a New Testament writing. Paul does not regard tongues as an embarrassing novelty but lists it as one of the gifts of the Holy Spirit: 'to one is given *through the Spirit* . . . various kinds of tongues' (1 Cor. 12: 8–10). Was Paul mistaken in regarding God as the author of the gift? If not, then how can something which is granted by the Author of 'every good and perfect gift' be regarded as an uncomfortable imposition with which the early church had to come to terms, but which we today can ignore with relief?

The gift was certainly being misused at Corinth, but this is precisely why Paul mentioned it in his letter to the church there and not in letters to other churches; it was the Corinthian church alone which was misusing the gift. Similarly the Lord's Supper is referred to by Paul only in the letters to the Corinthian church, certainly not because other churches were not observing it, but because at Corinth alone it was being misused. The impressive thing is that, however much the gift was being misused, Paul neither suggested that it was a spurious gift nor demanded that its exercise should cease. Paul's concern was not with discouraging the gift's exercise but with laying down principles concerning its proper function, its limitations and its orderly exercise. All of these suggest the continuance of the gift, not its disappearance.

Furthermore, it is not at all certain that the gift of tongues finds no mention in the New Testament Epistles apart from 1 Corinthians. Attention has already been drawn to the activity of the Holy Spirit in prayer described in Romans 8 and to the mention of 'spiritual songs' in Ephesians 5. A further suggestive pointer is found in verse 20 of the Epistle of Jude where the author writes, '*build yourselves up* on your most holy faith; *pray in the Holy Spirit*'. In view of Paul's equation already noted of speaking in tongues with praying in the Spirit, and in view of the connection Paul makes between speaking in tongues and self-edification (*i.e.* building up, see 1 Cor. 14: 4), we could infer that Jude is referring to this form of worship. Furthermore, in view of the fact that speaking with tongues was directly connected with the establishment of the churches of Jerusalem, Caesarea, Ephesus and probably Samaria it is hardly likely that this gift was unknown there when Paul wrote 1 Corinthians.

Such are the internal or biblical objections to speaking with tongues, and it cannot be claimed that they are very strong. Others have attacked and forbidden the exercise of the gift on the grounds of extreme emotionalism and fanaticism which they claim are associated with the gift. Such an association has at times occurred, but developments in the older churches of Christendom over the last twenty years have proved conclusively that there is no necessary and fundamental connection between tongues and fanaticism. This is increasingly recognized by denominational leaders. For example, the General Assembly of the United Presbyterian Church in the USA at its 1970 meetings gave cautious approval of the practice amongst its members, and stated that it 'should neither be despised nor forbidden'.

Some critics have attempted a psychological analysis and explanation of the phenomenon. They have pointed out that several non-Christian religions have something similar, and they have shown how something like tongues can be produced in certain emotional conditions in ways which no psychiatrist would have any difficulty in explaining. This is quite true and underlines the need always to distinguish between genuine and spurious manifestations. Basically, however, the objection brings us back once more to the question of the integrity and authority of Holy Scripture. Was Paul mistaken in asserting that there is a *genuine gift of the Holy Spirit* which enables Christians to pray, not in gibberish nor ecstasy, but in other languages? Were the apostles in Jerusalem mistaken in recognizing the gift of tongues to Cornelius and his household as such a marked evidence of the activity of the Spirit of God that they altered their fundamental approach to the admittance of Gentiles into the church? Was Luke mistaken in regarding the ability to worship in many languages and dialects on the day of Pentecost as a notable act of God marking the birth of the Christian church? If so, then the reliability and authority of the New Testament in matters of Christian faith and conduct are compromised and the New Testament documents become mere interesting historical and religious curios without any lasting validity and relevance.

On the other hand, as long as Christians accept the authority of the Bible in regulating their personal and corporate lives, there will be those who will seek the gift of tongues among other gifts and there will be others who will find themselves exercising this gift. When the gift is granted the important thing is that all Christians, whatever their denominational tradition or heritage, should control its exercise according to the principles laid down in Holy Scripture. Whenever they do that then God will be glorified and they and their churches will be edified.

Voluntary poverty

Earlier in the book we suggested that poverty, martyrdom and celibacy are three gifts described by Paul outside the main lists given in Romans 12, Ephesians 4 and 1 Corinthians 12, but that they are nonetheless spiritual gifts in the same sense as all the others to be exercised by some for the strengthening and edification of the church. This would appear to be so specifically in the case of poverty and martyrdom because they are included in Paul's whole discussion of the *charismata* which runs from the beginning of 1 Corinthians 12 to the end of 1 Corinthians 14 (see particularly 1 Corinthians 13: 3). Chapter 13 is not a separate sermon on love oddly placed in the middle of Paul's treatment of another subject; it is part of Paul's whole treatment of the subject of this book. Thus the inclusion of poverty and martyrdom in this material suggests that they are gifts in the same sense as all the others. This conclusion is underlined by the immediate context of 1 Corinthians 13: 3 which follows specific mention of the uselessness of speaking in tongues, prophesying and exercising the gifts of knowledge and faith (gifts all mentioned in the previous chapter) without love. Whether or not poverty and martyrdom have been recognized in modern times as *charismata*, they were certainly so recognized in the post-apostolic church.

In the earliest New Testament church voluntary poverty was particularly evident, for we read that all 'sold their possessions and goods' (Acts 2: 45) and 'as many as were possessors of lands or houses sold them' (Acts 4: 34). It is obvious, however, that this more or less universal exercise of voluntary poverty did not last long, for later we find Christians like Luke and Lydia with apparently considerable private means continuing to own their property. Later, in the Roman church, poverty became institutionalized and was required of all taking holy orders. There was a reaction against this at the time of the Reformation, but since then some Christians have exercised this gift, George Müller and C. T. Studd being amongst the most famous.

Those who exercise the gift of voluntary poverty and who thus give away all their possessions appear to do so for a variety of reasons. In the early church the incentive was to provide for the poor. When all who believed sold their possessions and goods they 'distributed them to all, as any had need' (Acts 2: 45). When as many as were possessors of lands or houses sold them, they 'brought the proceeds of what was sold and laid it at the apostles' feet; and distribution was made to each as any had need' (Acts 4: 34, 35). While God does not call all Christians to give away all their possessions He does charge them to remember those less fortunate than themselves and to give generously and sacrificially for their needs. 'Charge them . . . not to set their hopes on uncertain riches but on God who richly furnishes us with everything to enjoy. They are to do good, to be rich in good deeds, liberal and generous, thus laying up for themselves a good foundation for the future' (1 Tim. 6: 17–19).

Some Christians who have given away all they possess have done so, perhaps, because they have enjoyed great wealth or have found the lure of wealth so great that they have felt the only way to resist material temptation has been to become completely poor for Christ's sake. Some such reason as this would appear to have been behind our Lord's command to the rich young ruler to give away all he had (Mk. 10: 21). So great was his love of money that he would never have been able to follow the Lord while money remained in his pocket. C. T. Studd seems to have felt something like this about the fortune he inherited and which he subsequently gave away.

Yet other Christians have given away their possessions in order to prove the faithfulness of God. This was the motive behind George Müller's action in giving away his wealth and then establishing an orphanage without any assured means of income except the gifts of God's people. It was to prove that God would be God to the children in George Müller's care and would meet their every need. Possibly all of these motives will be present when a Christian exercises the gift of poverty. Suffice to say that God is no man's debtor, and all who become poor for Christ's sake because

God has called them to take such a step testify to the rich reward they receive as a result.

Perhaps in these days of unparalleled materialism there is a fresh need for the exercise of the gift of poverty. Rather surprisingly many Christians who are urging their fellows to rediscover spiritual gifts remain strangely silent where this gift is concerned. Unlike some gifts this one is most unspectacular when rightly exercised, for Jesus said to those who would give alms, 'do not let your left hand know what your right hand is doing, so that your alms may be in secret'. When this gift is rightly exercised only God will know, but 'your Father who sees in secret will reward you' (Mt. 6: 4).

Martyrdom

Martyrdom is the willingness and ability to endure death for the sake of Jesus Christ. A survey of Christian history, paying particular attention to the accounts of those who have died for their faith, emphasizes martyrdom's charismatic nature, for again and again it is obvious that those who die for their Lord often display characteristics of patience, of peace, of endurance under brutality and suffering, and of willingness to forgive those who are ill-treating them quite beyond their normal human expectations and capabilities. Thus Stephen was stoned without complaining and died praying for his killers, 'Lord, do not hold this sin against them' (Acts 7: 60). Only because he was empowered by the Spirit of God could he pray and die as he did. Only his vision of Christ in glory sustained him against the anger and bitterness of the Jewish Council (see Acts 7: 56). Similarly others down through the centuries have displayed superhuman powers as they have died for their faith in their Saviour.

One of the purposes of spiritual gifts, as has been seen, is to strengthen and build up the church and it is apparent from observation that martyrdom somewhat surprisingly has this result. One would expect the opposite to be the case, and certainly those who put Christians to death for their faith expect to destroy the church thereby and not to strengthen it. But the fact that martyrdom strengthens the church has been proved again and again throughout its long history.

The early church had a deeply moving custom of recording and relaying to other churches for their encouragement and challenge the dying words and deeds of martyrs in some particular outbreak of persecution. The day of their triumphant death was celebrated as the day of their birth. In early Protestantism, *Foxe's Book of Martyrs* was the staple diet of religious reading for thousands. The incomparably beautiful words and deeds of martyred Covenanters, for example, stirred Scottish Christianity to its depths. The African church in Uganda was planted by the martyrdom of its first English bishop and its first African converts. In the twentieth century examples abound from the jungles of South America to the prison camps of Siberia, from the Congo River to the remote mountains of Nepal. And invariably the result, sooner or later (and usually very quickly), has been a marked advance in Christian expansion.

The martyrdom of Stephen produced the church's first great wave of expansion as Christians from Jerusalem were scattered throughout the region of Judea and Samaria (Acts 8: 1) and as far as Phoenicia and Cyprus and Antioch. As a direct result, first Samaritans and later Gentiles were added to the original Jewish Christian community (see Acts 8: 4–25; 11: 19, 20). On another level the martyrdom of Stephen led to the conversion of Saul with all the far-reaching results that that entailed.

So the pattern has been often repeated. When Christians have been put to death for their faith others have fled from the area of persecution and established new churches elsewhere. At the same time non-Christians, among them sometimes those who have led the persecution, are converted and join the ranks of the church after seeing the way Christians have died. More than one world ruler has signed his own ultimate death-warrant by declaring war against the church, for the church is built on Christ, and the gates of hell, let alone earthly governments, cannot prevail against it (see Mt. 16: 18).

While, of course, Christians should never seek martyrdom they can have confidence that, if martyrdom comes, then God will give them the strength to endure it and to remain faithful to the end. They can also know that if they are called upon to die for their Lord, then their Lord will be glorified and the church will be strengthened for, as Tertullian said long ago, 'The blood of the martyrs is the seed of the church.'

Celibacy

Like poverty and martyrdom celibacy is a third gift mentioned in isolation from the main New Testament lists of gifts. It is a spiritual gift, for Paul says in connection with it 'each has his own *special gift* from God' (1 Cor. 7: 7). Similarly Jesus says of those who have 'made themselves eunuchs for the sake of the kingdom of heaven', 'He who is able to receive this, let him receive it' (Mt. 19: 12). Like poverty also this gift has become institutionalized within the Roman Catholic Church and is demanded of all who take holy orders. Protestants have naturally reacted against such demands and tend not to consider the place of the Christian celibate within the church. Yet Paul devotes some space to the subject in 1 Corinthians 7 and it is therefore necessary to consider his teaching.

In his first letter to the Corinthians Paul suggests that Christians are better single than married 'in view of the impending distress' (7: 26). What this was we do not know, although Paul must have been expecting some sort of cataclysmic upheaval, for he says 'the form of this world is passing away' (7: 31) and he warns that 'those who marry will have worldly troubles, and I would spare you that' (7: 28). Whatever trouble Paul was expecting, his advice does constitute a reminder that times will occur in human history when marriage will be less sensible than staying single. At the outbreak of the last war some Christians who were engaged to be married felt they should postpone their weddings until the upheaval of military service and damage from air raids, *etc.*, had passed. Times change and opinions about contemporary events vary too. There is no room for dogmatism here and different Christians will come to different decisions at one and the same time.

Paul also points out in 1 Corinthians 7 that unmarried Christians are freer to devote their time and energies to the Lord's service than married ones. 'The unmarried man is anxious about the affairs of the Lord, how to please the Lord; but the married man is anxious about worldly affairs, how to please his wife, and his interests are divided. And the unmarried woman or girl is anxious about the affairs of the Lord, how to be holy in body and spirit; but the married woman is anxious about worldly affairs, how to please her husband' (7: 32–34). Here is wise advice indeed! How many Christians have learned joyfully to accept the single state because of the opportunities for Christian service it provides! On the other hand Paul does not forget the advantages of marriage. Nor should we! It is all a question of balance and of each Christian exercising the gift granted to him or her from God.

Perhaps in these days, when sexual fulfilment is paramount in society and when single people are ostracized and often improperly suspected, Christians need to reflect again on Paul's teaching on marriage in this chapter. While the majority of Christians will continue to marry, others may find real peace in accepting that perhaps for a time, or even a lifetime, God would have them remain single that they may be spared worldly anxieties and may devote their whole lives to His service.

Contribution (*Rom. 12: 8*)

Besides the gifts we have examined so far, Paul includes two more gifts in his list in Romans 12 which, by their nature, are variously distributed among all church members. The first of these is liberal giving. 'Having gifts that differ according to the grace given to us, let us use them,' he writes: ' . . . he who contributes, in liberality; he who gives aid, with zeal; he who does acts of mercy, with cheerfulness' (Rom. 12: 6, 8).

Only a few Christians, comparatively speaking, will probably be called to exercise the gift of voluntary poverty, literally giving away all their earthly possessions out of love and service to Christ; many more, indeed all Christians, are expected by the New Testament writers to contribute financially, according to their means, to the ongoing work of the church. The amounts different Christians give and the spheres to which they give will vary. Some will direct most of their gifts into their local church funds. Others will give to specific evangelistic, missionary or social and charitable agencies as God directs them. More important, the proportion of their incomes which different Christians give will vary. Many take a tenth or tithe as a norm by which to work, but others are enabled, by the Holy Spirit, to give much more. Those who thus exercise this gift often pass unnoticed and unthanked by other Christians for, as was mentioned earlier, true Christian giving should always be anonymous (see Mt. 6: 2–4).

Liberal exercise of the gift of contribution brings its own deep reward. The Word of God promises that 'he who sows bountifully will also reap bountifully' (2 Cor. 9: 6), and the bountiful reward comes as the giver finds that, despite his generous giving, possibly to the point of his own poverty, God continues to meet his needs and to make further contribution possible. In addition the giver rejoices that the needs of others are being met and God is being thanked thereby. The giver's own Christian life is enriched as his righteousness is increased and his worship of, and devotion to, God are deepened (see 2 Cor. 9: 6–15).

Moreover, contributing 'in liberality' may affect much more than mere money. Sometimes the giving of cash to some comfortably distant cause may even be an escape from responsibility rather than an acceptance of a challenge. The world has shrunk. Modern communications bring the people of the world to our doorstep. Overseas students in Western universities represent almost every nation to which European missionaries once went. Political changes or the tragedy of war make the arrival of refugees and displaced persons in a friendly country a regular event. At the same time many of the young people of our own lands feel estranged from society. The hippie, the drop-out, the drug-addict, the drifter, is still someone embraced by the love of God and the terms of the gospel. Is there not a need for a truly charismatic attitude of liberal giving in these circumstances? What may have to be contributed, and therefore sacrificed, is our furniture and carpeting when it is worn out by a crowd of young people, our time and energy and compassion when we are seeing an addict through 'withdrawal', our respectable image in the neighbourhood when 'strange types' are given hospitality in our home. Something valued and perhaps only painfully released will have to be 'contributed' if churches and individual Christians are to be the first to welcome and assist an Asian refugee, for example, or the first to offer help to a family whose son has been arrested for a cruel crime. There are some churches where a Christian may 'contribute' a good deal of his popularity or reputation for 'balance' if he invites to tea, and then to church, the long-haired or those of a different race or colour. Yet such contribution is desperately needed today if Christianity is even to be credible in some areas of life. Surely those who are called to such a ministry are in the charismatic succession of those who in the early church sold what they possessed and laid it at the apostles' feet, and those who a little later earned the amazed comment, 'See how these Christians love one another!'

86

Acts of mercy

Last in his list of gifts in Romans 12 Paul cites the doing of acts of mercy. 'Blessed are the merciful,' said Jesus (Mt. 5: 7), thereby indicating that His followers were to show kindness and compassion to others in a careless world. Paul makes it clear that the ability to give of one's time and energy to help people in need comes every bit as much from the Spirit of God as the ability to preach effectively, or to heal the sick or to speak in tongues or to exercise any of the other spiritual gifts listed in the New Testament. Equally the quiet performance of acts of mercy is every bit as vital to the church's health and completeness as the exercise of what might be thought of as the more spectacular gifts. Indeed, so often it is the spontaneous, sacrificial helping of people in need which does as much or more in bringing them to Christ as the evangelistic sermon in a crowded arena.

The precise difference between 'liberal giving' and 'acts of mercy' is not clear. Both will require a vision of the need, a heart touched with compassion, and a willingness to act. Perhaps the 'acts of mercy' were the specifically organized movements of social help which distinguished the early church so clearly from the brutal and heartless society in which it grew. We read of the 'daily distribution' to widows in Jerusalem (Acts 6: 1) and the famine-relief fund in Antioch (Acts 11: 27–30). Paul carefully organized the fund for poor Jewish Christians: gifts were collected from the Gentile churches, and care taken with the appointment of delegates to gather and deliver the funds. The Antioch collection was a response to prophecy. The Jerusalem distribution was organized so as to recognize the prior task of apostleship. Paul's fund was seen as a vindication of his evangelism. So again the more spectacular and the more mundane gifts intermingled and were interdependent.

In today's situation there is still need for the voluntary church relief organization. In Britain, such organizations as

Christian Aid and Tear Fund perform prodigies of relief and mercy in the name of Christ. Other countries have similar organizations. For their continued ministry they need not only the generous contribution of the average Christian, but the dedicated effort of the Christian called to administer and organize their work – often at a salary much lower than his abilities could claim elsewhere.

Though in Britain and some other countries the Welfare State has become responsible for great areas of work once pioneered by Christians, there are many gaps in the provision made. The approach to drug addiction is an outstanding example. The church has led the way in warning of its growing danger and Christians in many parts of the world have pioneered efforts to cure and rehabilitate the addict. The aged, the homeless, the sufferers from more obscure diseases, the blind, the mentally handicapped: all of these needy people unite in a cry for the divinely-motivated 'work of mercy' at the personal and the organizational level.

Finally, Government-sponsored welfare-work, which in some countries is so much a part of modern life, offers wide scope for the exercise of this rôle. We are convinced that Christian probation officers, Christian social workers, Christian doctors and nurses can all contribute something to this sphere of service which a non-Christian who knows nothing of the energizing power of the Holy Spirit cannot offer. There is much talk of ministering to the whole man in modern society, but without endowments from the Holy Spirit, neither the worker nor his work is truly whole. Again, it will have to be recognized that many such tasks offer less financial return than the worker might hope to receive in other professions. There is great need for well-qualified young Christians to consider the call of God, the sacrifice involved, the strains imposed, and the mental and spiritual demands made, in such acts of mercy.

'He who does acts of mercy,' says Paul, should do so 'with cheerfulness' (Rom. 12: 8). He or she may well pass unnoticed by others, may be rarely thanked for help taken for granted, and will certainly face the temptation to lapse into a professionalism or a condescending attitude which has produced the expression 'as cold as charity'. But a cheerful spirit in such circumstances, warmed with genuine humanity and interest, will constitute a real demonstration of the power of the risen Christ.

Helpfulness and compassion are becoming increasingly rare in our selfish and acquisitive society. Christians must not be slow in making up what others lack, with a readiness to emulate the Good Samaritan and to hasten willingly to the help of others in need.

5 DANGERS WITH SPIRITUAL GIFTS

The New Testament makes no secret of the fact that, despite their divine origin and their evident value to the church, spiritual gifts can be misused and abused, and the Christian's understanding of their place and function in the church can be mistaken, with consequent harmful results. This is because Christians, although partakers of the Holy Spirit, remain human and imperfect in this present life, always prone to error, always needing to strive for full knowledge, complete holiness and total union with Christ their Lord.

The Holy Spirit is gentle and gracious. He can be grieved by sinful actions and His influence can be quenched by wrong attitudes. He does not swamp and submerge the personality of the Christian. Certainly He does not 'possess' the Christian in the way that a spiritualist medium is invaded and dominated by some spirit-force. This is one of the fundamental differences between genuine spiritual experience granted by God and occult experiences which result from dabbling in forbidden things. The Christian is still himself, and is in control of himself. His own will, his own prejudices, his own convictions, are always ingredients of what he does, even when seeking to serve God in the power of the Holy Spirit. Sometimes his prayers will be wrongly motivated; sometimes in prayer he will ask for the wrong things; and sometimes in public prayer he will express himself ungrammatically. Although he is spiritually engaged, his own personality defects and social background will be evident in what he does. The same is true of every area of Christian activity, and it is an expression of the loving condescension of God that He should be willing to employ in His noble service such weak and mixed-up creatures as we all are.

The exercise of spiritual gifts is no exception. How can it be otherwise? Because some of them are unusual, and because they are so emphatically initiated by the Holy Spirit, it is possible to forget this. We can fall into the error of thinking that a prophecy, or a 'tongue', or a prayer for healing have something so supernatural about them that it would be impious to question them or to submit them to any test. Yet clearly the Christian's own limitations, prejudices and mixed motives can be operative here as in any other area of service. The Corinthian Epistles underline this repeatedly. Although they were exercising genuine spiritual gifts, the Corinthian converts nevertheless brought over into their exercise tendencies from their nationality and culture. A Greek tendency to exalt eloquence and worldly-wisdom, a carelessness about morality that was proverbial in this sea-port, and a confusion between prophecy and the exciting and ecstatic activities associated with the pagan 'oracles' – all of these were intermingled to a greater or lesser degree with their exercise of spiritual gifts. It could happen then, and it can happen now.

Nevertheless, the possibility that gifts may be misused or their place in the church misunderstood is never allowed by the New Testament writers to constitute a reason for their exclusion from Christian lives and fellowships. Rather, difficulties associated with the exercise of the *charismata* are squarely faced, so that Christians may be alive to possible dangers and thereby able to avoid them.

Spurious gifts

Right at the beginning of his whole discourse on the *charismata* in 1 Corinthians Paul recognizes that Christians are in danger of exercising gifts which are completely false and counterfeit and which do not have their origin in the activity of the Spirit of God. 'No one', he says, 'speaking by the Spirit of God ever says "Jesus be cursed!" ' (1 Cor. 12: 3). Quite why some of the Corinthians were making this strange acclamation while sincerely believing they were under the influence of the Holy Spirit is difficult for us to understand. Perhaps they had misunderstood Christian teaching about Christ having become a curse in His death on the cross (see Gal. 3: 13) and were thus mistakenly saying 'Jesus be cursed!' If this were so, then their error was human only, and such 'gifts' as they were exercising were the product of purely human endeavour. Or maybe some of the Corinthians were still under the control of spirits from their heathen past (see 1 Cor. 12: 2) in which case their 'gifts' were more sinister, evil copies of the true.

Whatever the explanation of 1 Corinthians 12: 3, Paul's words are a salutary reminder to all Christians that, even when they are acting with the best of intentions and the utmost sincerity, their work might not be as spiritual as they might imagine. Significantly, however, Paul does not make the presence of counterfeit manifestations in the church at Corinth a reason for the exclusion and prohibition of all charismatic activity. That some gifts are false constitutes no argument for their disuse but rather the opposite. In avoiding false gifts Christians should strive to exercise genuine gifts. And how can they do this? 'No one can say "Jesus is Lord" except by the Holy Spirit' (1 Cor. 12: 3). Here is a timeless yardstick to apply to the exercise of every gift. If the impression gained from seeing gifts exercised is primarily one of noise or emotional excitement; if those exercising gifts seem more concerned with promoting the idea of their own holiness, or spirituality, or ability than with exalting the Lord Jesus Christ; if gifts are seen as a means merely of inducing personal thrills, then Christians will be fully justified in doubting their reality.

Here is a constant, humbling challenge to the Christian seeking or exercising gifts. Does such a Christian desire gifts in order that he may better proclaim Jesus as Lord? In exercising his gifts can the Christian honestly claim that his sole desire is the uplifting and displaying of Christ? The example of John the Baptist, already quoted, bears repetition in this connection. When he began to realize that his days as a prophet were drawing to an end and that his consequent influence in the life of his country was coming to its close, he was not jealous for his position, or his power, or the continuance of his gift of prophecy, or the allegiance of his friends. Instead he rejoiced that, as he decreased, Christ increased. Would that all who exercise gifts from the gracious hand of God always did so with the same humble, healthy motives as he who was called to announce the coming of the Messiah!

Discouragement and jealousy

Secondly, Paul recognizes in 1 Corinthians 12 that, when gifts are exercised within a church or fellowship of Christians, some Christians might easily become discouraged because they do not exhibit the same gifts they see in others. In their discouragement they might become jealous and resent their apparent poverty where gifts are concerned.

This in fact is a frequent problem in Christian groups. Some Christians become discouraged because they do not enjoy great preaching ability, or because they do not seem to be able to win others with ease and regularity. Not that this sort of discouragement is always their own fault. Those well endowed with these kind of prominent gifts do not always help. Some such Christians have been known to castigate others for their seeming failure in various areas of their lives where only certain spiritual gifts can lead to success, and not all Christians possess these gifts.

In 1 Corinthians 12 Paul warns against discouragement at the absence of some much-desired ability. Really, he says, this kind of thinking shows failure to understand the true nature of the church. The church is a body, and like any living body needs all sorts of different members, performing different functions, for its health and perfection. All the members cannot be the same, doing the same things, enjoying the same gifts. Discouragement at lack of gifts is rather like a foot saying it does not belong to the body because it is not a hand, or an ear making the same complaint because it is not an eye (verses 15, 16). A body would soon be in difficulties if its various members were capable of that kind of independent thought and action. Jealousy at the gifts possessed by others shows equal ignorance of the nature of the church, for 'if the whole body were an eye, where would be the hearing? If the whole body were an ear, where would be the sense of smell?' (verse 17). Inevitably, some gifts, such as evangelistic preaching, teaching or public speaking in tongues, do give their possessors more prominence than do others, such as quietly administering the day-to-day business of the church, or giving liberally and anonymously from one's financial resources. But then, some parts of an ordinary body, such as the speech organs, the eyes and the hands are more prominent than internal organs whose regular but unseen functioning is vital to the body's health. If Christians constantly bear in mind that they are all members of the body of Christ, and therefore have different functions to perform, then discouragement and jealousy of others should be avoided.

Selfishness and pride

As some may become discouraged and jealous when gifts are exercised, there is an equal danger that others may become selfish and proud of the gifts they possess. They may overrate their own particular gifts and come to disparage others who only possess what they consider to be lesser gifts. Self-styled 'specialists in evangelism', for example, may start criticizing other Christians as 'unspiritual' because they honestly cannot say that through them God is bringing others to conversion and new birth. Others who claim to be specially gifted in personal counselling may attempt to make hasty diagnoses of situations without troubling to ascertain the actual facts and without recognizing the faithful and prayerful help being offered by people on the spot. Even worse, enthusiasts who believe they are called to exorcize may claim to recognize demon possession on quite inadequate grounds, causing unnecessary distress to those involved. In extreme cases some Christians may demand that all others exercise certain gifts as a mark of their total commitment to Christ, or even in some very extreme cases of their commitment to Christ at all. The demand made by some that all Christians should have a post-conversion experience called 'the baptism of the Holy Spirit' which must always be marked by the gift of speaking in tongues is, we believe, an example of this error; hence our full examination of this teaching in the following section.[1]

Paul makes it very clear in 1 Corinthians 12 that this kind of thinking, as with discouragement and jealousy, demonstrates a total misconception of the nature of the church. 'The eye cannot say to the hand, "I have no need of you," nor again the head to the feet, "I have no need of you" ' (verse 21). When the body of Christ functions as it should all the gifts will be exercised. But Paul makes it very clear that the exercise of one or more gifts by all Christians is not demanded, nor should it be expected.

Disorder and confusion

A third danger which comes when gifts as such are specifically recognized and encouraged lies in their exercise in conditions at variance with the nature of God Himself, and hence displeasing to Him. That this had happened at Corinth when Paul wrote his first letter is very obvious from chapter 14. Too much emphasis was being placed on speaking with tongues and not enough on prophecy (verses 1–5). People were praying in tongues without their prayer being interpreted (verses 27, 28). Several people were praying in tongues and prophesying all at the same time (verses 27–31). In the midst of all this commotion, the women in the congregation were maintaining an incessant chatter, or interrupting speakers if they did not understand what was being said (verses 34, 35).

[1] See pp. 133ff.

The whole pattern of Christian worship at Corinth was in confusion and Paul does not hesitate roundly to criticize the Christians there for the abuses they were tolerating if not encouraging.

In view of this very clear description of the way gifts were being misused at Corinth, it is sad and surprising that similar abuses and excesses have been tolerated within some churches and Christian fellowships in modern times. Obviously charismatic worship can be and often is orderly and restrained. But it is sadly true that many, many Christians have rejected the benefits which the exercise of spiritual gifts can bring because of unhappy and disturbing experiences they have suffered. If those who exercise the *charismata* want other Christians to take them seriously when they claim that their worship follows the New Testament pattern, they must make every effort to be above reproach where such abuses are concerned.

The nature of God

In warning the Corinthians to avoid dangers associated with spiritual gifts Paul directs them first to a consideration of the nature of God. The abuses they were tolerating in their worship were quite out of harmony with God's desire for order and peace. 'God is not a God of confusion but of peace', he says (14: 33). Thus the women should be quiet and ask their husbands what they did not understand when they get home. Prophets should prophesy one by one, not all at the same time. Only two or three people should speak in tongues in any one meeting and each time their prayers must be interpreted. On the whole the Corinthians should keep their praying in tongues for their own private devotions where it is most valuable. Rather than going to church meetings with a desire to speak in tongues they should go with a desire to prophesy, for prophecy builds up the church. Indeed a desire for edification as opposed to demonstration should be uppermost in their minds when they assemble for worship. When this desire is coupled with orderly behaviour then the church will be strengthened. Paul's last words to the Corinthians on the whole subject of gifts is that 'all things should be done decently and in order' (14: 40).

As far as the Corinthians' comparison and over- or under-evaluation of each others' gifts was concerned, Paul reminds them of the sovereignty and the sovereign purpose of God for the church. Because the church is a body its members have different functions to perform for the health and well-being of the whole. Gifts exist to enable the different functions to be fulfilled. These gifts, says Paul, are distributed according to God's sovereign purpose. To one is given one gift, to another a different gift. 'All these are inspired by one and the same Spirit, who apportions to each one individually *as he wills*' (12: 11). 'As it is, God arranged the organs in the body . . . that there may be no discord in the body' (12: 20, 25).

God's sovereign distribution of gifts thus means that not all Christians will exercise the same gifts, nor should they expect so to do. Paul obviously considered this point of supreme importance, for he specifically makes it twice in 1 Corinthians 12, once at the beginning of the chapter and once at the end. On the first occasion he lists nine gifts and makes it clear that these are distributed among different Christians *according to the will of the Spirit*. Nowhere does Paul suggest that any of these nine gifts is more important than any other or that it will be distributed with greater frequency than any other (see verses 4–11). On the second occasion Paul gives another list and then rhetorically asks, 'Are all apostles? Are all prophets? Are all teachers? Do all work miracles? Do all possess gifts of healing? Do all speak with tongues? Do all interpret?' (verses 29, 30). His unwritten but clearly implied answer is, 'No, of course not!'

The need for love

As a further antidote to the abuse of spiritual gifts Paul stresses the need for love on the part of all for all. Because the church is a body, suffering or disorder in one member affects all the other members, just as a small illness like toothache or a boil can make the whole body feel sick. God desires the members to have the same care for one another so that 'if one member suffers, all suffer together; if one member is honoured, all rejoice together' (1 Cor. 12: 25, 26). Where members of a church are discouraged, or jealous, or selfish, or proud in their exercise of gifts this kind of loving care cannot exist between them. Yet for Paul it is essential if abuse of gifts is to be avoided.

Right in the middle of Paul's whole section on spiritual gifts in 1 Corinthians comes his sublime exposition of love. Chapter 13 must not be considered in isolation from chapters 12 and 14, for it is central to their theme and was always intended by Paul to be understood in the context of gifts. Desire for love is a higher desire than the desire to exercise gifts. Gifts exercised without love only irritate and annoy (verse 1). God's purpose will never be achieved through the exercise of gifts unless they are exercised in love (verses 2 and 3). 'Love is patient and kind' (verse 4), so it does not disparage those lacking in gifts but waits God's time for gifts to be given. 'Love is not jealous' of the gifts of others, or 'boastful' of its own (verse 5); 'it is not arrogant or rude. Love does not insist on its own way' (verse 5), demanding from others what God Himself does not demand; 'it is not irritable or resentful' (verse 5) if God works through gifts in ways which do not square with its own preconceived ideas; 'it does not rejoice at wrong' when gifts are abused and misused, 'but rejoices in the right', always pleased when it sees gifts exercised in accordance with the teaching of Scripture (verse 6).

'Love never ends' (verse 8). One day all the gifts will pass away, their purpose served, but in that day love will endure. Make love your aim then, says Paul, and, when you are sure you are doing that, then you may earnestly desire the spiritual gifts. There can be little doubt that, had gifts been exercised in a greater spirit of love in Corinth and in more recent times, some of the excess which has so often characterized their employment might well have been avoided.

II THE BAPTISM OF THE SPIRIT AND SPIRITUAL GIFTS

6 BAPTISM OF THE SPIRIT: THE PROBLEM

Why is the subject of spiritual gifts regarded as so controversial and divisive? That it is so regarded is beyond question. At every level of Christian life and service examples can be found of dispute and discord amongst fellow-Christians. At the denominational level this has resulted in the formation of separate churches with distinctly charismatic emphases and characteristics. Within missionary societies controversy has raged and missionary candidates have sometimes been required to commit themselves on one side or the other. Among local churches of all types there have been examples of the fellowship being split into charismatic and non-charismatic factions. In non-church groupings such as school and college Christian Unions the subject regularly becomes an issue. The darkness of the picture should not be exaggerated, and it would be far from true to say that the subject is automatically divisive. Yet sufficient harm is done for the problem to be a serious one. If the supernatural element in the Christian church is as clearly taught in Scripture as this book maintains, why cannot Christians agree in recognizing it to be so?

Two things have made Christians in the twentieth century hesitant and suspicious of those who have exercised spiritual gifts and both of these have been mentioned already in this book. The first has been connected with frequent excesses which have often accompanied the exercise of the more spectacular gifts such as speaking with tongues and the healing of the sick. In this connection we have suggested that abuse is no argument for disuse but rather calls for right use. But the second stumbling-block has been more serious, for it has been concerned with the Christian's understanding and interpretation of the New Testament as a whole, and it is to this that of necessity we must now turn.

Until very recently almost all Christians in the Western world who have advocated the exercise of spiritual gifts have done so in the context of a spiritual experience called 'the baptism of the Holy Spirit'. They have claimed that the New Testament teaches that the work of the Holy Spirit in the Christian believer is twofold. First, there is His work in regeneration whereby the individual is convicted of sin, repents and believes in Christ for salvation. Secondly, there. is His work in 'baptism' whereby, after regeneration, the believer's life is raised to a new level of holiness and the believer is empowered for service. Just as all who would receive salvation must be born anew, so all who have been born anew must subsequently seek the baptism of the Spirit if their lives are to become fully pleasing to God.

Associated with the baptism of the Spirit has been the gift of speaking with tongues. There have been varieties of opinion here but, broadly speaking, it has been held that speaking with tongues is the spiritual gift always granted as evidence that the baptism of the Spirit has taken place. This gift has thus been exalted above all the other gifts and has been described as the gateway to their exercise. Without the baptism of the Spirit evidenced by speaking with tongues, it has been asserted, no Christian life can be fully effective nor can other gifts of the Spirit be rightly exercised.

Even when excesses have not characterized the exercise of gifts, many Christians have been uneasy with this teaching. They have doubted its scriptural basis; they have noted its divisive effect in creating categories of first- and second-class Christians (those who have 'received the baptism' and those who have not); and they have been unable to avoid pointing to Christians in both ancient and modern times, obviously full of the power of the Holy Spirit in their personal lives and effective service, yet unaware, either of the gift of tongues, or of a 'second experience' of the Holy Spirit in the manner indicated. Unfortunately, when many such Christians have concluded that Scripture does not teach such a clearly defined and necessary work of the Holy Spirit, they have all too hurriedly rejected clear scriptural teaching on the exercise of spiritual gifts as well, and this to their own and often their associates' spiritual detriment.

Is division, then, unavoidable? Must Christians become polarized into two groups: those who are baptized in the Spirit and who thus exercise spiritual gifts, and those who are not so baptized, and therefore reject spiritual gifts? The writers of this book believe that such a polarization is tragic and unnecessary. To underline our position we shall lay side-by-side the two most commonly-held views of the baptism of the Spirit, examine them sympathetically and measure them beside the wider teaching of the New Testament. In doing so, we cannot avoid touching on controversial matters, but we believe that this can be done without rancour and with a genuine recognition of both the strength and weakness of various opinions, and a glad acknowledgment of the genuine devotion and sincerity of Christians holding different views. We shall seek to show, first, that very real theological difficulties are involved, but secondly, that the exercise and enjoyment of God's gifts in the church do not in fact depend on the complete resolution of these difficulties.

The advocates of the theory of a twofold work of the Holy Spirit and its necessary association with speaking with tongues find scriptural support for their teaching mainly in the experiences of Christians as recorded in the Acts of the Apostles. First, attention is drawn to the original one hundred and twenty disciples of Jesus including the apostles themselves. In Acts 1, the reasoning goes, these men and women, who were undoubtedly Christians (for they believed that Jesus was the Messiah and had been raised from the dead), were nevertheless powerless and inept in their decisions as they waited for the promised Holy Spirit. On the day of Pentecost these same people were 'filled with the Holy Spirit' (Acts 2: 4). They gave immediate evidence of this by speaking in tongues; they witnessed boldly of the resurrection and three thousand converts were added to the church. Subsequent chapters of the Acts describe their continued powerful witness in the face of severe opposition.

It is concluded that, just as there was a point in the experience of the apostles when they were Christians without the power of the Holy Spirit, so Christians today can be in the same situation. Just as the apostles spoke in tongues when they were filled with the Holy Spirit, so modern Christians will speak in tongues when they receive the baptism of the Spirit. Just as speaking in tongues was the gateway for the apostles to the exercise of all the other gifts as described in later chapters of Acts, so speaking with tongues will open the door to all the other gifts for modern Christians.

Following the experience of the apostles themselves further support for the theory is drawn from the experience of the Samaritan converts recorded in Acts 8. Here is another group of people, it is said, who are obviously Christian, for 'they believed . . . and were baptized' (verse 12). Yet the Holy Spirit 'had not yet fallen on any of them, but they had only been baptized in the name of the Lord Jesus' (verse 16). When Peter and John 'laid their hands on them . . . they received the Holy Spirit' (verse 17). Speaking with tongues is not specifically mentioned but obviously occurred because when Simon, the bogus convert, 'saw that the Spirit was given through the laying on of the apostles' hands, he offered them money, saying, "Give me also this power, that any one on whom I lay my hands may receive the Holy Spirit" ' (verses 18, 19). What could it have been that would have attracted Simon, the erstwhile magician, if it had not been the ability to convey the power to speak in tongues? Here is supposedly clear proof of a distinction between regeneration and the reception of the Holy Spirit, clear witness that the initial evidence of the presence of the Holy Spirit in a believer's life is speaking with tongues, and a clear example of the laying on of hands being used to bring about the baptism of the Spirit.

Next, appeal is made to the experience of the apostle Paul in Acts 9. The reasoning is that he was converted on the Damascus Road, and three days later received the Holy Spirit when he was visited by Ananias who laid his hands on him (verse 17). Although the Acts record does not specifically state that Paul spoke in tongues on this occasion, it is concluded that he obviously did because in 1 Corinthians 14: 18 he says, 'I thank God that I speak in tongues more than you all.' The pattern, it is claimed, which is seen in the experience of Paul is the same as in every other instance recorded in the Acts: first, conversion, second, baptism in the Spirit, third, speaking with tongues.

Similar conclusions are drawn from the experience of Cornelius and his family and friends in Acts 10. The passage does not provide evidence of the post-conversion nature of the baptism of the Spirit, for it is obvious that its occurrence here is simultaneous with conversion, or nearly so. But the passage does supposedly provide a clear example of speaking with tongues demonstrating evidence of baptism with the Holy Spirit, for it was only when Peter and the believers with him heard Cornelius and the others speaking thus that they realized the Holy Spirit had been given.

Perhaps the favourite passage of those who advocate a second experience of the Holy Spirit evidenced by speaking with tongues comes in Acts 19, where it is recorded that on reaching Ephesus Paul 'found some disciples. And he said to them, "Did you receive the Holy Spirit when you believed?" And they said, "No, we have never even heard that there is a Holy Spirit." And he said, "Into what then were you baptized?" They said, "Into John's baptism." And Paul said, "John baptized with the baptism of repentance, telling the people to believe in the one who was to come after him, that is, Jesus." On hearing this, they were baptized in the name of the Lord Jesus. And when Paul had laid his hands upon them, the Holy Spirit came on them; and they spoke with tongues and prophesied' (verses

1–6). What clearer evidence could there be of the twofold work of the Holy Spirit? it is asked. Here is a group of men, obviously Christians, for they are called 'disciples', yet who did not possess or even know about the Holy Spirit. When they received the Holy Spirit they gave evidence of the same by speaking with tongues. In the same way, it is reasoned, there are large numbers of Christians today who have not received and are largely ignorant of the Holy Spirit. When they do receive Him the normal pattern observable in the early church will result; they will speak in tongues.

With these passages in Acts is linked 1 Corinthians 12–14. It is reasoned that, although the baptism of the Spirit as an experience subsequent to conversion is not specifically mentioned in connection with these chapters, it is nonetheless assumed. Does not Paul say, 'I want you all to speak in tongues' (14: 5), and 'do not forbid speaking in tongues' (14: 39)? In fact, it is said, the three chapters are addressed only to those who have been baptized in the Spirit after their conversion, for 12: 1 should not read 'Now concerning spiritual gifts', but 'Now concerning those who are spiritual'; and 'those who are spiritual' are those who speak with tongues, and those who speak with tongues are those who have been baptized with the Spirit. Paul's implication in 12: 10 and 12: 30 that not all speak with tongues refers, it is argued, to the public as opposed to the private exercise of the gift. God does not intend all to speak with tongues in church meetings, but He would have all baptized with the Spirit and evidence this by speaking in tongues.

Yet further support for this pattern of teaching is drawn from Mark 16: 17, 18: 'And these signs will accompany those who believe: in my name they will cast out demons; *they will speak in new tongues*; they will pick up serpents, and if they drink any deadly thing, it will not hurt them; they will lay their hands on the sick, and they will recover.' Jesus Himself, it is asserted, made it clear that speaking in tongues would be part of the normal experience of all those with full faith in Himself.

Some modern writers are now drawing on passages from

the writings of prominent Christians of earlier days as added support for their understanding of Scripture. In *As at the Beginning* Michael Harper traces a line from Tertullian and Augustine of Hippo in the early church, through such Puritans as Thomas Goodwin in the seventeenth century, to prominent Christian leaders of the nineteenth century like Charles Simeon and D. L. Moody, in an attempt to show that present-day emphases are not so new in Christian thinking as some might like to suggest. It certainly cannot be denied that throughout church history there has been a line of teaching which has favoured a twofold work of the Holy Spirit expressed in a variety of ways.

This, then, is a summary of much modern teaching on the gifts of the Spirit. The gifts of the Spirit, it is said, are received through the baptism of the Spirit. Those so baptized demonstrate their baptism by speaking with tongues. Speaking with tongues is the gateway into the exercise of all the other gifts. If Christians would exercise gifts they must first seek and receive the baptism.

Scriptural evidence for this teaching appears impressive. Famous names from church history can be called in support. But is it right? And if it is not right does it matter?

It must be recognized immediately that such an interpretation is at variance with the understanding of very many Bible scholars, theologians, and Christian leaders whose loyalty to the Scriptures is unquestioned and unqualified. They present a theology of the Holy Spirit which calls in question that just outlined. They compel us to face at least the possibility that the theological position under discussion is confused and faulty at several points.

If this is so, then the practical excesses sometimes seen in the exercise of spiritual gifts may spring, not merely from an excess of enthusiasm or a lack of emotional balance, but from a more basic cause. In that case, it would not be sufficient to take steps to minimize or eliminate the excesses (as is being done admirably in many circles today) while leaving the doctrine in confusion. If doctrine is at fault, and the fault leads to excesses, then there will always be the danger that those who are enthusiastic for the exercise of spiritual gifts will fall back into the excesses which they rightly seek to avoid. Moreover, those Christians whose theological position differs from that outlined may well react against the gifts themselves, associating them completely with beliefs which they cannot share. It is our conviction that this is precisely what has often happened, to the detriment of all. We must therefore now examine the doctrine of the baptism of the Spirit in more detail.

7 THE NEW TESTAMENT POSITION

Principles of scriptural interpretation

Teaching associated with the subject of the baptism of the Holy Spirit and speaking with tongues as outlined in the previous chapter raises the issue of the method whereby Scripture is to be understood and interpreted. The whole force of the argument there recorded rests on the assertion that the experiences of certain individuals and groups as recorded in the Acts of the Apostles were intended by God to be normative in their precise details for all Christians for all time. Thus it is legitimate to construct doctrine upon them.

This basic assertion that the Acts records are in themselves sufficient for the formulation of Christian doctrine without supporting evidence from the rest of the New Testament must be questioned. For when pressed, advocates of the position outlined have to admit that, although Jesus gave detailed teaching on the Person and work of the Holy Spirit, as for example in John 14–16, He was silent on the work of the baptism of the Holy Spirit as they understand it. Equally, the New Testament Epistles, although again often concerned with the Person and work of the Holy Spirit, do not expound the doctrine of the baptism of the Holy Spirit as a post-conversion experience, nor do they connect it with speaking in tongues, nor do they ever urge their readers to seek such an experience.

The experiences of some individuals recorded in Acts are,

of course, intended to be normative for all Christians until Christ returns. But where this is so there is ample supporting evidence both from the teaching of Christ and the apostles. It is obvious from the New Testament that, to enter the kingdom of heaven, a man must be born anew; but this is obvious not because Acts tells of certain people who were born anew, but because Jesus said, 'You must be born anew,' and, 'unless one is born anew, he cannot see the kingdom of God' (Jn. 3: 7, 3). To expound a major New Testament doctrine from the experiences of individuals alone, however valuable and valid those experiences may have been to the individuals concerned, is a highly doubtful practice which can result in all kinds of problems and difficulties.

Suppose, for example, we maintain that the way in which the first followers of Jesus received the Holy Spirit is in every detail intended to be the way God would have all Christians receive the Holy Spirit at some point after their conversion. If the apostolic experience is normative then the results of the apostolic experience must be normative as well. Besides devotion to apostolic teaching, fellowship, breaking of bread and prayers, those baptized with the Holy Spirit in the manner of Acts 2 must have all things in common and sell their possessions and goods and distribute them to all, as any have need (Acts 2: 44, 45). They must not meet to worship God in church buildings specially erected for that purpose, but must meet for worship in their homes and in the nearest Jewish place of worship (Acts 2: 46; 3: 1). The authors have not heard of any who have carried their interpretation of apostolic example to these lengths!

The account of the conversion of Saul of Tarsus is another case in point. On the evidence of Acts 9 alone, it might be imagined that an essential ingredient of conversion is a dramatic meeting with Christ which prostrates a man on the ground and causes him to lose his sight. It is the doctrinal sections of the New Testament which put this in perspective, disentangle the fundamental issues from the special and incidental details, and define Saul's conversion (and ours) as a turning from all self-effort and self-righteousness to an attitude of trust in, and surrender to, the once-crucified and now-risen Christ.

New Testament doctrine can be formulated only after due consideration has been made of the whole of its teaching on a particular subject. Its recorded experiences of individuals must then be related to this. Doctrine cannot be formulated from individual experiences and then imposed on the rest of the New Testament framework. If a correct understanding of New Testament teaching on the subject of the baptism of the Holy Spirit and its relation to speaking with tongues is to be reached, the didactic sections of the New Testament (that is, Christ's teaching in the Gospels and the apostles' teaching in the Epistles) must be considered first. To these, experiences of groups and individuals can then be related and interpreted.

It is an understandable temptation to anyone who has had a particularly vivid experience resembling one described in the Bible, to reverse this method – to begin with the Acts experiences and then try to understand the teaching of Christ and the apostles in their light. Such a Christian, however, is putting his understanding at risk and treating the Bible in a manner which he probably would not apply to its teaching on other subjects which he cordially holds in common with all Christians. It is here that the misunderstanding and separation begin, to everyone's loss.

The silence of the Epistles

We have already[1] noted that, when we turn to the didactic parts of the New Testament, and especially the Epistles, in search of a second experience of the Holy Spirit, we are confronted by a remarkable absence of material. There is much about the Person and work of the Holy Spirit, of course, but it is difficult to find any references to a division

[1] See p. 109.

between two groups of Christians, those 'baptized in the Spirit' and those not so baptized.

In his letter to the Romans, for example, Paul sets forth in logical sequence his understanding of Christian doctrine, and in chapter 8 he deals with the Holy Spirit. He speaks of two basic 'lifes', 'life in the flesh' and 'life in the Spirit' (verses 1–8). He says that possession of the Spirit is the distinctive mark of every Christian (verse 9). As a result every Christian is guided by the Spirit (verse 14), assured of his divine sonship by the Spirit (verses 15–17), and enjoys a foretaste of glory by the Spirit (verses 18–24). The Spirit also helps the Christian in prayer (verse 26). Nowhere, however, does Paul speak of a 'second experience' of the Holy Spirit which the Romans had had, or should have. Nor does he mention speaking with tongues in connection with such an experience. It really is inconceivable that, if such a second experience of the Spirit was as necessary to Christian experience in the New Testament era as many would have us believe, Paul should fail to discuss it in this context.

The same conclusion must be reached in connection with Paul's Letter to the Ephesians which similarly deals in some detail with the work of the Holy Spirit within the believer. Paul speaks of the Christian having been 'sealed' with the Spirit (1:13). This is the 'guarantee' of his inheritance (1: 14). The Holy Spirit gives access to the Christian through Christ to the Father (2: 18). Christians, built together into the church, are 'a dwelling-place of God in the Spirit' (2: 22). The Holy Spirit is the Author of Christian fellowship (4: 3) and has granted gifts to the church as a consequence of the Ascension (4: 7–11). In all of this there is no mention of a 'second experience' of the Spirit. As in Romans 8 Paul neither reminds the Ephesians that they have had such an experience nor does he urge them to seek one. Rather, they must take care not to grieve the Holy Spirit (4: 30) and they must 'go on being filled with the Spirit' (5: 18 – literal translation).

This absence of teaching about a second experience of the Spirit in Ephesians is even more striking than in Romans, since much of Ephesians is concerned with God's gifts to the church, and with the weapons of warfare provided for spiritual conflict. Surely, if the gift of tongues is as necessary to the exercise of other spiritual gifts as some would have us believe, Paul would have carefully spelled out the connection in his Ephesian Letter.

There is in fact simply no place in any of the Epistles where any teaching is given about a 'baptism of the Spirit' distinct from the Holy Spirit's work in conversion and regeneration. Those who advocate such a baptism really must grasp that this is the serious theological reason for the rejection of their teaching by many earnest Christians. Such Christians are not hiding from something clearly taught in Scripture because of unbelief, or fear, or prejudice. Their devotion to the whole Word of God compels them to treat with great reserve a line of teaching which may be one possible interpretation of some incidents in Acts when considered in isolation, but which seems to have no theological backing in the rest of the Bible.

Baptism with the Spirit

If, then, there is strong reason to doubt that the New Testament teaches a second experience of the Spirit incumbent on all believers, it is fair to ask what the New Testament does teach on the controversial subject of the baptism of the Spirit. The occurrence of the phrase itself is in fact rare, occurring only in the ministry of John the Baptist, once in the ministry of Jesus, once in the ministry of Peter and once in the writings of Paul.

Mark's Gospel describes John the Baptist as the one sent to prepare the way for the Lord, and goes on to tell how he 'appeared in the wilderness, preaching a baptism of repentance for the forgiveness of sins. . . . And he preached, saying, "After me comes he who is mightier than I, the thong of whose sandals I am not worthy to stoop down and untie. I have baptized you with water; but *he will baptize you with the Holy Spirit*" ' (Mark 1: 1–8). Matthew's and Luke's Gospels describe John's ministry in similar terms. Jesus' reference to baptism with the Spirit in Acts 1: 5 recalls John's baptism with water and forecasts His apostles' imminent baptism with the Holy Spirit. Peter's mention of baptism with the Spirit is nothing more than a recollection of Jesus' words on the subject: 'And I remembered the word of the Lord, how he said, "John baptized with water, but you shall be baptized with the Holy Spirit" ' (Acts 11: 16). Paul links baptism with the Spirit with the unity of all Christians within the church when, in 1 Corinthians 12: 13, he says, 'by one Spirit we were all baptized into one body'.

From these passages it appears that baptism with the Holy Spirit is a distinctive work of Christ. It does something which John (and presumably all who went before him, for John was the greatest born of woman – Mt. 11: 11) could not do. It thus adds to human experience what was unknown before Christ began so to work.

This 'baptism with the Holy Spirit' was anticipated in the Old Testament. All the Old Testament prophets bewailed the disobedience of Israel and her failure to keep God's revealed law. Some of the prophets looked forward to the day when God would act in a new way to bring about the obedience He had so long desired. The means He would use would be the Holy Spirit. Ezekiel wrote, 'A new heart I will give you, and a new spirit I will put within you; and I will take out of your flesh the heart of stone and give you a heart of flesh. *And I will put my spirit within you*, and cause you to walk in my statutes and be careful to observe my ordinances' (Ezk. 36: 26, 27). Jeremiah also anticipated the same situation when he wrote, 'Behold, the days are coming, says the LORD, when I will make a new covenant with the house of Israel and the house of Judah . . . I will put my law within them, and I will write it upon their hearts; and I will be their God, and they shall be my people . . . I will forgive their iniquity, and I will remember their sin no more' (Je. 31: 31–34). It was this new covenant Christ came to make (Mt. 26: 28). It was this 'new Spirit' Christ came to impart. It was this new baptism Christ came to give.

If this second line of approach is followed, then 'baptism with the Holy Spirit' will be regarded as one New Testament description among many of the change which God works in the life of an individual when he or she becomes a true Christian and is thus incorporated into the body of Christ. This change produces holiness of character and power for service. It comes, in normal circumstances, not through prayer and the laying on of hands, but through repentance toward God and faith in our Lord Jesus Christ. With this Paul's teaching agrees. 1 Corinthians was written, not to those who had been baptized with the Spirit at some time after their conversion, but 'to those sanctified in Christ Jesus, called to be saints together with all those who in every place call on the name of our Lord Jesus Christ' (1 : 2). Addressing these, later in the letter, Paul says, 'By one Spirit we were *all* baptized into one body – Jews or Greeks, slaves or free – and *all* were made to drink of one Spirit' (12 : 13). Paul is here obviously equating the Corinthians' baptism with the Spirit with their setting apart for Christ's service, with their calling to be saints, with the time they began to address Jesus as Messiah and Lord. Baptism with the Spirit is not a second experience, therefore, but an initial experience whereby an individual becomes a true Christian. In New Testament times it was evidenced, not by speaking in tongues, although that sometimes occurred, but by baptism in water whereby public recognition was given by the individual in the act of joining the church to something which had already spiritually taken place.

Even the teaching of Acts 2, rightly understood, supports this view. After the original disciples had received the Holy Spirit on the day of Pentecost Peter preached to the pilgrims who were thronging the temple forecourts in Jerusalem. He claimed that the outpouring of the Spirit which had just occurred had begun to fulfil the prophecy of Joel. He related it to the life and death of Christ, charged the crowd with responsibility for the crucifixion, and announced the resurrection and glorification of Jesus. The crowd was deeply affected. In despair they cried, 'Brethren, what shall we do?' Peter replied, 'Repent, and be baptized every one of you in the name of Jesus Christ for the forgiveness of your sins; and you shall receive the gift of the Holy Spirit' (verse 38). It is inconceivable that Peter is here promising a different measure of the Spirit to the one he and the other disciples had just received. Their reception of the Spirit, for reasons which will be shown later, was abnormal. Peter here expounds the normal way the Spirit is received and he links it indivisibly with conversion; the Spirit is received through repentance and baptism in the name of Jesus. Baptism with the Spirit is not a second experience reserved for some. It is the universal experience of all true Christians. 'By one Spirit we were *all* baptized into one body' (1 Cor. 12: 13).

One further point must be made. In the passages just referred to no necessary connection between baptism with the Spirit and speaking with tongues is demanded. With the exception of Mark 16: 17, which will be discussed later,[2] Jesus never taught about speaking with tongues, neither did the apostles demand it as a necessary sign that the Spirit had been received. There is no mention of the three thousand converts of Acts 2 speaking with tongues, although, as has been seen, they received the Holy Spirit; nor of the lame man in Acts 3, nor of the five thousand converts in Acts 4, nor of the Ethiopian eunuch in Acts 8, nor of the converts at Antioch in Acts 11, nor of the many converts won on Paul's first missionary journey (Acts 13, 14), nor of Lydia and the Philippian gaoler in Acts 16. Yet it is recorded that all these were baptized in water. This was the necessary sign of baptism with the Spirit. Speaking with tongues, when it occurred, was significant and worthy of mention, but was by no means necessary in the earliest Christian communities as evidence that the Spirit had been given.

[2] See pp. 129f.

8 INTERPRETING THE ACTS EXPERIENCES

In the previous chapter we have suggested that, according to New Testament teaching, the baptism of the Spirit is not an experience subsequent to conversion but the initial conversion experience itself whereby an individual becomes a true Christian and is spiritually admitted into the fellowship of Christ's church. We have suggested that there is no necessary connection between this experience and speaking with tongues, although speaking with tongues sometimes accompanies the experience and sometimes follows later. If these conclusions are correct, what is to be made of passages in the book of Acts, earlier referred to, which, as interpreted in the manner there indicated, suggest the opposite? Central to the theme of the last chapter was the assertion that the experiences of individuals recorded in Scripture must be related to scriptural teaching as a whole, and not the other way round. If this is borne in mind when the Acts experiences are considered, it quickly becomes apparent that these experiences do not necessarily support the post-conversion view of the baptism of the Spirit and certainly need not be evaded by Christians who hold a different view.

The day of Pentecost (*Acts 2*)

In Acts 2 the first disciples do indeed seem to have been real Christians with a knowledge of the crucified and risen

Lord as Saviour, yet without the fullness of the Holy Spirit. Peter's confession at Caesarea Philippi (Mk. 8: 27–30), the faith of Peter and John at their discovery of the empty tomb (Jn. 20: 8), Christ's impartation of the Holy Spirit in the upper room on the first Easter Sunday (Jn. 20: 22) and Thomas' acclamation of Jesus as Lord and God (Jn. 20: 28) all point to the conclusion that some, if not all, of the hundred and twenty disciples who were filled with the Holy Spirit on the day of Pentecost were already regenerate in the full New Testament sense of the word. Being regenerate then, they were subsequently 'baptized' or 'filled' with the Holy Spirit (Acts 1: 5; 2: 4) in an experience which was both dramatic and meaningful in the highest sense of the words. We suggest, however, that their experience was quite abnormal rather than normal, because of the historical period in which they lived.

We live two thousand years after the completion of the historical work of Christ. They lived while Christ's work was actually in progress. Because the apostles' lives spanned the historical crucifixion, resurrection and ascension of Christ and the outpouring of the Holy Spirit, inevitably they knew Christ before they knew the Holy Spirit. If it is valid to reason from this that Christians today can know Christ without knowing the Holy Spirit, it is equally valid to reason that Christians can enjoy the benefits of the death of Christ without knowing anything about the benefits of His resurrection, for that must have been the apostles' condition at a previous stage. Similarly someone can be a true Christian merely because he sees in Christ an example to follow without seeing any necessity for faith in the benefits of His death, for that too must have been the apostles' condition at a still earlier stage in their experience. Such reasoning of course is patently false because it does injustice to New Testament teaching about the nature of a true Christian. According to the New Testament a true Christian is one who, aware of the New Testament record of the life, death, resurrection and ascension of Christ, exercises faith in Christ and receives the Holy Spirit. The New Testament tells us how the closest friends of Christ became Christians in this sense, but it does not suggest that everybody else must follow the stages of their experience in every minute detail in order to qualify as Christians. Neither can a doctrine of the baptism of the Holy Spirit as a necessary second experience following conversion be drawn from the apostles' experience as recorded in Acts 2.

Indeed, there is evidence in the New Testament that the apostles themselves did not regard their baptism with the Spirit as a necessary post-conversion experience but as part of their total experience of Christ which, in others, as far as the details were concerned, could be altered, foreshortened and condensed. Some years after the historic day of Pentecost, when justifying to the Jerusalem church his baptism of Cornelius and his household, Peter recalled his own and the other disciples' experience of the Holy Spirit on that day. He reasoned that it was because Cornelius had so obviously received the Holy Spirit as they had that he had gone ahead with baptism. Indeed, he equated Cornelius' experience of the Holy Spirit with the apostles' on the day of Pentecost (see Acts 11: 15), and he described the experience as 'baptism with the Holy Spirit' (see Acts 11: 16). Then, in Acts 11: 17 Peter concluded, 'If then God gave the same gift to them as he gave to us *when we believed in the Lord Jesus Christ*, who was I that I could withstand God?' By describing his Pentecostal experience in these terms Peter is saying that this was part of his total salvation experience. For Peter the day of Pentecost was the culmination of three years in the presence of the Saviour. Yet what God worked in Peter over the course of three years He apparently worked in Cornelius in the space of half an hour! Thus Peter himself disclaims any attempt to force others into the detailed straitjacket of his own experience where the baptism and fullness of the Spirit are concerned.

The Samaritans (*Acts 8*)

If the experience of the apostles does not support a necessary post-conversion view of the nature of the baptism of the Spirit, what of the experience of the Samaritans in Acts 8? Here undoubtedly were people who had responded to the proclamation of the gospel and had been baptized, yet on whom, we are specifically told, the Holy Spirit had not fallen (verse 16). Surely, if one group of people could be Christians without possessing the Holy Spirit, then it must follow that others can be in the same condition.

In considering this admittedly difficult chapter it must be understood, first of all, that Philip's mission to the Samaritans with resulting large numbers of conversions was highly significant in the history of the early church. Viewed against the background of the centuries of racial and religious hatred which had separated Jews from Samaritans it was remarkable that the early Christians, who were still all Jews at this time, should even carry the good news to Samaritans at all. When large numbers of Samaritans responded as they did to Philip's preaching, there was an immediate danger that a separate Samaritan church would be formed, divided by traditional racial hostility from the Jewish church in Jerusalem and Judea. It was apparently to avoid this eventuality that God, in His sovereignty, ordered events in the unusual way recorded by Luke.

That it was unusual for converts to be baptized without receiving the Holy Spirit seems apparent from the way in which Luke draws attention to the situation (verses 15, 16). That the Holy Spirit was withheld from the Samaritan converts until Peter and John arrived and laid hands on them would appear to have been God's way of showing both the Jewish and Samaritan Christians that, although they had hitherto been estranged by bitter racial and religious hatred, they were now members of one body, the body of Christ. The new Samaritan converts were made to realize their need of the mother-church at Jerusalem. In turn the hesitant leaders at Jerusalem were compelled to acknowledge the reality of the Samaritans' conversion. Once again the whole situation was highly abnormal, and New Testament doctrine cannot be built on isolated abnormal incidents.

Furthermore, it must be said that speaking with tongues is not specifically mentioned in the Samaritan context. Simon's offer of money to Peter for the gift of imparting the Holy Spirit would seem to suggest that there was some tangible evidence that the Spirit was given with the laying on of apostolic hands. This evidence might well have been speaking with tongues, but the silence of Scripture on the issue advises against dogmatism either way.

Paul's experience (*Acts 9*)

As has been shown earlier, some Christians reason that Paul was converted on the Damascus Road and received the baptism of the Spirit from the laying on of Ananias' hands three days later, when at the same time he spoke with tongues. Paul's own recollection of the whole affair, however, as recorded in Acts 22, does throw this interpretation of the events into serious doubt. That Paul both saw and heard the Lord on the Damascus Road is clear. That this traumatic experience shattered his earlier convictions is equally clear. But is the picture of a blinded man fasting for three days and nights, unforgiven and unbaptized, the picture of one born anew of the Spirit of God? Is it not rather a picture of one mentally and physically broken, groping in agony for reality in the face of shattered illusions? To this tormented man Ananias did come with the laying on of hands that he might be filled with the Spirit. But Ananias also came with the advice, 'Rise and be baptized, and wash away your sins, calling on his name' (Acts 22: 16). Surely this is advice to someone in need of conversion, and the fact that Paul took Ananias' advice and thereafter 'took food and was strengthened' (Acts 9: 19) points to the conclusion that, in so doing, he was converted and at the same time was filled with the Spirit. Paul's experience followed the norm of New Testament teaching. His conversion and his filling with the Spirit were not two separate experiences but one, both aspects of which gave meaning to the other.

Furthermore, it really is unreasonable to link Acts 9 with 1 Corinthians 14 where Paul says, 'I thank God I speak in tongues more than you all,' and to conclude from this that Paul spoke in tongues when Ananias laid hands on him. That Paul spoke in tongues is not surprising since, as was shown earlier, speaking in tongues is one normal form of Christian prayer which God gives to some for their edification. But to link together Acts 9: 17 and 1 Corinthians 14: 18 and to claim that the latter sprang from the former is quite unjustified.

Cornelius' experience (*Acts 10*)

Consideration in part has already been given to the Cornelius incident in the discussion on Acts 2. It is the story of a group of people entering the Christian life for the first time, and the exercise of 'tongues' and 'prophecy' is related to their conversion, not to a subsequent experience.

Just as Acts 8 tells of the first Samaritans who became Christians, so Acts 10 tells of the first Gentiles who became Christians. If it was a breakthrough when Philip visited Samaria, it was even more of a breakthrough when Peter entered the Roman military complex at Caesarea. That his reluctance so to do was overcome only by the direct intervention of God Himself in two remarkable dreams simply demonstrates the height and strength of the barrier which separated Jew from Gentile during the first century. At this time Jews utterly despised Gentiles, and Gentiles were utterly scornful of Jews in return. To the Jews, Gentiles were beyond the pale of God's mercy and any contact with them, purposeful or accidental, cut off an offending Jew from the worshipping community. If there was a danger when Samaritans were converted that they would become a separate Samaritan church, there was a far greater danger when Gentiles were converted that their conversion would pass unrecognized by the Jewish church. Hence the manner of Cornelius' conversion. Hence the presence of Jewish-Christian observers from Jerusalem who were able to support Peter during the subsequent criticism he encountered for going to Cornelius and thereby breaking Jewish law. Hence the speaking with tongues on the part of Cornelius, his relatives and friends. It is obvious from the discussion recorded in Acts 11 that it was only the repetition at Caesarea of the day of Pentecost manifestation which persuaded the Jewish Christians of the reality of the Gentiles' conversion and of Peter's rectitude in administering baptism. Again the Cornelius incident, like the Samaritan incident, was abnormal and special, and it is for that reason that it is so carefully recorded.

Twelve men at Ephesus (*Acts 19*)

All this leaves only the incident of the twelve men at Ephesus recorded in Acts 19. Here, as with Paul in Acts 9, the case for the post-conversion nature of the baptism of the Spirit rests on the assumption that the men in question were Christians before they received the Holy Spirit. Yet it is just this assumption which is most seriously open to question. Paul's careful questioning of them suggests, indeed, that the men were not only ignorant of the existence of the Holy Spirit (verse 2) but apparently somewhat ignorant of important aspects of the ministry of Jesus as well (verse 4)! If we assume, as many do, that they had been influenced by the preaching of Apollos (18: 24; 19: 1), this idea is strengthened, for Apollos, though 'instructed in the way of the Lord' and 'fervent in spirit', knew only John's baptism and needed to understand 'the way of God' more perfectly (Acts 18: 25, 26). That Paul apparently felt it necessary to baptize the men in the name of the Lord Jesus (verse 5) surely provides further evidence that they were not true Christians at all prior to this encounter. That they received the Holy Spirit as part of their baptismal ceremony (verse 6) is again further evidence of the close connection the early Christians saw between conversion and reception of the Holy Spirit. That they spoke in tongues and prophesied (verse 6) is an interesting and significant fact which again links spiritual gifts with conversion rather than with a later experience.

It is also worthy of attention that, as with the Samaritans and Cornelius' Gentile group, a threat to the unity of the early church was removed by this incident. Charles Scobie[1] has shown that during the first century a fairly widespread 'John the Baptist sect', which was in its turn part of a much more general Jewish sectarian movement, existed in countries where Jews were numerous. Emphasis on repentance, baptism and preparation for the Coming One were characteristic of this movement. It is highly probable that the twelve men at Ephesus belonged to this 'John the Baptist sect'. It was obviously important that their relationship with the newer Christian movement should be regularized and understood. In Acts 19 Luke is inferring that disciples of John who had moved no further were half-way to being Christians; the Christian gospel was the fruition of their hopes and beliefs. Therefore, when given the opportunity, they should embrace Christ by faith, receive Christian baptism and enter into the experience of the communion of the Holy Spirit. Luke thus commends the men at Ephesus who so readily carried their incomplete faith to its logical and spiritual conclusion. Too much should not be read into Luke's description of the men at Ephesus as 'disciples'. Quite apart from all that has been said, this does not necessarily mean they were Christians, for the term is used elsewhere by Luke to describe followers of John and of the Pharisees.

---

[1] Charles Scobie, *John the Baptist* (SCM, 1964).

Summary

Reception of the Holy Spirit and speaking with tongues are explicitly connected on three occasions in the Acts of the Apostles: on the day of Pentecost, at the home of Cornelius and at Ephesus. They are also implicitly connected on one other occasion, the conversion of the Samaritans. No connection is implied in the conversion experience of Paul. With the exception of our Lord's own disciples and the Samaritans in Acts 8, reception of the Holy Spirit is integral to the conversion experience, and is not a second experience subsequent to conversion. On all four occasions when reception of the Holy Spirit and speaking with tongues are explicitly or implicitly connected, groups of people, not individuals, are concerned. Hence it is doubtful exposition to use these incidents today to press personal experiences on individuals following the pattern of any one of them. All four occasions when speaking with tongues occurred affected the unity of the church. At Pentecost, the unity of Christians within the body of Christ was symbolized and expressed. The church was publicly recognized as a distinct entity in the Jewish nation, preaching its message, practising its ordinances, and receiving new members. In Samaria, Caesarea and Ephesus three communities with particular problems which threatened the continued unity of the church were integrated in an unmistakable way. Each was a special occasion. To say this is not to dodge the possible requirement of the New Testament for a personal baptism of the Spirit for all Christians by imagining special circumstances. The whole context of each story underlines how special it is. In our view Acts, like the rest of the New Testament, does not support the teaching of those who would urge all Christians to a necessary experience of the baptism of the Holy Spirit subsequent to their conversion. Neither does it link speaking with tongues to such a necessary experience.

9 INTERPRETING FIRST CORINTHIANS

Besides their particular interpretation of passages in Acts those who encourage Christians to seek a further baptism of the Holy Spirit after their conversion appeal to Paul's First Letter to the Corinthians in support of their position and in support of the inseparable connection between the baptism of the Spirit and speaking with tongues.

'Those who are spiritual' (*1 Cor. 12: 1*)

We drew attention earlier to this alternative translation of this verse instead of the more normal words 'spiritual gifts'. From this alternative translation it is concluded that 'those who are spiritual' are those who have been baptized with the Spirit since their conversion and have consequently spoken in tongues. It is only to such, it is said, that chapters 12–14 are addressed. Thus Paul clearly recognized the existence of two types of Christian in the Corinthian church – those who had been baptized with the Spirit, and those who had not.

To reach such conclusions from one alternative translation of one verse in all of Paul's letters would really seem to be forcing exegesis out on to a dangerously weak limb. 'Those who are spiritual' is a fair alternative translation to 'spiritual gifts', or 'spiritual things', but translators are surely conveying the meaning of the Greek words in their context when they translate them 'spiritual gifts'. In any case, as we shall reason later, 1 Corinthians elsewhere teaches that there is no necessary connection between spirituality and the exercise of gifts, so even if the alternative reading were to be preferred it would hardly support the conclusions outlined.

'I want you all to speak in tongues' (*1 Cor. 14: 5*)

Appeal is made to this verse to support the view that God would have all Christians speak in tongues, and those who argue in this way conclude that Christians who do not thus speak are inevitably missing out on God's best for their lives. An immediate difficulty in the way of this conclusion lies, of course, in the verse's apparent contradiction of 1 Corinthians 12: 10 and 30 where Paul clearly suggests that speaking with tongues is a gift given to some and not to others. This apparent contradiction is reconciled by saying that the references to speaking in tongues in chapter 12 refer to the public exercise of the gift, whereas the verse in question in chapter 14 refers to its private exercise. God would have all speak in tongues for their private edification, it is said, but only some in meetings for the edification of the church.

Paul obviously does distinguish between the private and public exercise of tongues in 1 Corinthians 14 and we drew attention to this distinction in chapter 2. This distinction does not apply to this verse, however, for it can be maintained only at the cost of separating half the verse from its other half and all the verse from its context. In this verse Paul is speaking about the public exercise of tongues, for he is comparing tongues with prophecy – 'he who prophesies is greater than he who speaks in tongues, unless some one interprets, so that the church may be edified'. Whatever Paul may be recommending in this verse, it is certainly not privately praying in tongues. Furthermore it must follow that if Paul is saying here that all should speak in tongues he is also saying that all should prophesy. 'I want you all to speak in tongues but (I want you all) even more to prophesy' is the clear import of his words. It is inconceivable that Paul can in fact be saying this and thus contradicting himself so soon after stating very firmly that the Holy Spirit singles out particular individuals for the gift of prophecy (12: 10) and asking the question 'are all prophets?' (12: 29).

Is Paul guilty, then, of flagrant self-contradiction, or do his words have reasonable meaning? The answer to the problem probably lies in considering it against the background of the whole situation in which 1 Corinthians was written. Paul wrote this letter largely to correct abuses which were rampant in the Corinthian church. The church's moral standards were all at sea (chapters 5, 7). Party spirit was creating bitterness and division within the community (chapter 1). Decency and order in worship left much to be desired. Celebrations of the Lord's Supper had become gluttonous orgies (chapter 11). Spiritual gifts were being exercised in an atmosphere of confusion. In church meetings everybody was speaking in tongues and prophesying at the same time (chapter 14). Christians were unhealthily comparing the value of their gifts, and speaking with tongues was held in over-high regard.

It is this latter situation which Paul is addressing in chapters 12–14. Because spiritual gifts were being abused at Corinth Paul does not make this a reason for prohibiting their exercise. 'Do not forbid speaking in tongues,' he says; 'but all things should be done decently and in order' (14: 39, 40). In other words the answer to misuse is not disuse but right use. And one way to use the gifts correctly is to hold a balanced understanding of their value. Prophecy is a more valuable gift than tongues because it edifies the church. The main value of tongues lies in their private exercise where they edify the individual (14: 2, 4, 14). In church, tongues are valueless unless accompanied by interpretation (14: 5). Those who customarily speak with tongues need not, indeed must not, cease, although they must learn to control themselves. But they would do better, when going to church meetings, to go with a desire to prophesy than to speak with tongues.

When Paul says, 'I want you all to speak in tongues, but even more to prophesy,' he is not laying down an eternal theological principle but is speaking to those in the habit of exercising these gifts. At Corinth these would appear to have constituted a majority of church members. It is vital to realize that in 1 Corinthians 12 and 13 Paul is setting forth the theology of spiritual gifts and in 1 Corinthians 14 he is applying that theology to the specific Corinthian situation. Chapter 14 must be interpreted by chapters 12 and 13 and when this is done the apparent contradiction between 14: 5 and 12: 10, 29, 30 disappears.

With this conclusion that 'you all' in 14: 5 refers, not to all Christians, but to those who in fact exercise the gift, a literal translation of the Greek agrees. The force of Paul's words, when literally translated, is not simply, 'Now I want you all to speak in tongues,' but 'I want you all to go on speaking in tongues', or 'I want you all to continue to speak in tongues'. The point is, the English sentence 'I want you all to speak in tongues' implies obligation. It means, 'I want you all to speak in tongues, because I think you should.' But the English sentence 'I want you all to continue to speak in tongues' does not imply the same obligation but suggests instead an acceptance of the 'status quo' with a recommendation that it be maintained. Thus understood it becomes clear that the 'you all' of 'I want you all to continue to speak in tongues' should be regarded as referring to those who already speak in tongues. It is not a general exhortation addressed to all Christians in every age.

Other support for speaking in tongues

Of Scriptures used to support the view that all Christians should speak in tongues it only remains to examine Mark 16 : 17, 'And these signs will accompany those who believe . . . they will speak in new tongues.' All modern translations of the New Testament relegate the whole section (verses 9–20) to a footnote as none of these verses is found in the earliest extant manuscripts. This makes doubtful any conclusions drawn from them. But if the passage is taken at its face value, two points are immediately apparent.

First, the promise refers to 'those who believe' (verse 17).

The people in mind are those who respond with faith and baptism to the preaching of a gospel which distinguishes between the saved and the lost (verse 16). There is no suggestion of a post-conversion experience.

Secondly, 'speaking in new tongues' is listed with casting out demons, protection from snakes and poisons, and the healing of the sick (verses 17, 18). Clearly all Christians do not have such experiences: it is a list of the kind of dramatic thing which will in fact sometimes accompany the preaching and believing of the gospel. The Acts of the Apostles records examples of most of these incidents; more recent history records others. But the passage neither commands all Christians to do these things nor says that they ought to have similar experiences.

If scriptural support for the idea that all Christians should speak in tongues is weak, so is evidence drawn from the writings of outstanding Christians of former or modern times. All that such evidence shows is that, from time to time, prominent Christians have supported a particular interpretation of Scripture. Their prominence alone, however impressive, must never of itself be allowed to validate their conclusions. The knowledge of all Christians, even the best, is but partial (see 1 Cor. 13: 12). Hence it is the duty of Christians of each and every generation to study the Scriptures for themselves, to give due consideration to the beliefs and conclusions of others who have gone before, but to seek with the aid of the Holy Spirit to be guided into all truth.

On the issue under discussion we have sought to set the relevant Scriptures in their context. A recognition of the sad results which have followed when Christians have followed particular schools of interpretation at the expense of the clear teaching of Scripture should encourage, among all Christians, a humble willingness to re-examine the whole Word of God, and a whole-hearted determination to be slow in condemning those whose understanding and experience differs from their own.

10 RESULTS OF MISINTERPRETATION

Confused teaching inevitably gives rise to confused practice. Although we have distinguished between the extremes which have often characterized the exercise of spiritual gifts in recent times and the doubtful theological foundation which has often been used to justify the exercise of such gifts, these two things are in fact inseparably connected. This is why a careful understanding of the whole New Testament teaching on the place and exercise of gifts is essential if abuses are to be avoided. For as long as the foundation is dubious, a church or fellowship will always be in danger of falling into excess in practice even if excess is corrected or eliminated for a while. In our view a number of serious results can follow from the idea that the baptism of the Spirit attested by speaking with tongues is a post-conversion experience to be sought by all Christians if their lives are to be holy and their service effective.

A false emphasis

Perhaps the most serious result of the post-conversion idea of the baptism of the Spirit lies in the way it can draw attention away from the work of the Holy Spirit in regeneration. Because it is the experience of the baptism of the Spirit which produces a new standard of holiness and a new fire in service, it becomes the paramount experience for which regeneration is only a preparation.

It is sad to see how this conclusion is often tacitly, and sometimes explicitly, reached in the writings of those who advocate this post-conversion nature of the baptism of the Spirit. Conversion itself is seen very much in terms of a human decision – a hand is raised, a card is signed, or assent is given to a Bible text. And often this is admitted to achieve very little. It is only when the convert is later baptized with the Spirit that he gains victory over sin, or release from some degrading vice, or healing from some deep-seated personality problem.

On the other hand the New Testament teaches that Christ came that men might have life and might have it to the full. Christ gives living water which a man may drink and never thirst again. If any man is in Christ he is a new creation. The New Testament writers rejoice, not that their readers have been baptized with the Spirit since their conversion, but that they have been 'born anew to a living hope through the resurrection of Jesus Christ from the dead' (1 Pet. 1: 3). It is this which produces holiness of life. It is this which calls forth sacrifice in service. It is because of this that they possess 'a spirit . . . of power, and of love, and of a sound mind' (2 Tim. 1: 7, AV).

Division

Secondly, the idea that the baptism of the Spirit is a post-conversion experience inevitably creates division between Christians, for it unavoidably draws a line between the ordinary Christian and the 'Spirit-baptized' Christian, between the Christian ignorant of the gift of tongues and the Christian who speaks in tongues. The divisions which have resulted in churches and Christian fellowships where a group has adopted this teaching and has then over-enthusiastically sought to force it on their fellows must have caused much grief to the Holy Spirit. Yet such division over the exercise of gifts is completely unnecessary once the connection with a post-conversion baptism of the Spirit experience and the supremacy of tongues as the gateway to the other gifts are removed. When gifts are placed within the setting of the church and their distribution is recognized as lying absolutely within the sovereign will of God, such unholy division should pass away.

Necessity to speak in tongues

Thirdly, the inseparable connection which is often made between baptism with the Spirit and speaking with tongues makes it inevitable that sooner or later desire for the baptism of the Spirit becomes in fact a desire to speak in tongues, and all kinds of stratagems are adopted in order to produce the desired manifestation. Tongues become the great be-all and end-all of Christian life and discipleship. Those who encourage all their fellow-Christians to seek the gift of tongues seem to have learned, probably by trial and error, that something akin to speaking with tongues can often be induced in the right kind of mental state and emotional atmosphere. Hence their prayers and fasting for the conferment of the gift, hence the noise and frenzies of some of their 'receiving-in' meetings.

We read with alarm of the same Christians receiving repeated layings-on of hands in order that they might receive the baptism of the Spirit. Yet Jesus said, 'If you then, who are evil, know how to give good gifts to your children, how much more will your Father who is in heaven give good things to those who ask him!' (Mt. 7: 11). If baptism with the Spirit and speaking with tongues is the paramount experience its advocates claim, there should be no need for this kind of repetitive urging and seeking.

This needs to be underlined, for great harm can be done to unbalanced people, oversensitive people, and those who have an unhealthy desire for the dramatic or the mysterious. Most Christian leaders have sooner or later the experience of counselling and helping some Christian who has got into mental agony, sleeplessness or despair, because of this kind of pressure. Many more have met others whose emotional imbalance and nervous idiosyncrasies have become greatly exaggerated by the same pressures, sometimes to the point of breakdown. Yet others have persuaded themselves that some self-induced phenomenon was the baptism of the Spirit, only to find before long that 'it didn't work' – a discovery which led them not only to doubt that experience but to doubt the whole Christian gospel. Naturally, every responsible and compassionate Christian leader would disown any practice which clearly produced such results. But a false emphasis will often do precisely this, even though the Christian who creates the emphasis may not wish it to happen.

A false yardstick of spirituality

When gifts in general and tongues in particular are linked inseparably with the baptism of the Holy Spirit, it further follows that the presence or absence of gifts (generally the more dramatic ones are in mind) becomes the yardstick of spirituality. Those who exercise such gifts are those who are spiritual, while those with no such gifts are unspiritual. Indeed, we have shown how this conclusion is reached from an alternative translation of 1 Corinthians 12: 1. Yet this is most dangerous teaching. Gifts are not self-authenticating. The mere presence of something seemingly supernatural or dramatic proves nothing, otherwise there would be no need to test apparent gifts by the Word of God and the exercise of love (1 Cor. 13). The Corinthian church was 'not lacking in any spiritual gift' (1 Cor. 1: 7) yet Paul had to admonish its members, 'I, brethren, could not address you as spiritual men, but as men of the flesh, as babes in Christ,' and 'you are still of the flesh' (1 Cor. 3: 1, 3).

This is a fundamental point, and needs to be remembered by those who exercise the more dramatic gifts, by those who are troubled by their own lack of such gifts, and also by those who reject the whole charismatic emphasis because of the mistakes of some of its adherents.

First of all, the possession of an exciting gift does not imply that one has reached maturity. Nor does it imply that one has received what God is most anxious to give. Rudeness to other Christians, the discourteous pressing upon them of one's own experience, the barely-concealed pleasure felt in hinting darkly at startling anecdotes, impatience with a fellow-Christian who does not spring to an admiring reception of one's alleged word of knowledge, suggestions that a group, or committee, or church needs to 'open up to God', to 'stop quenching the Spirit', *etc.*: these are not minor faults to be dismissed as mere excess of enthusiasm. They are examples of that impatience and unkindness, boastfulness and rudeness, insistence on one's own way and rejoicing in wrong which Paul outlines in 1 Corinthians 13 as being denials of love. And he insists that love is the utterly supreme and glorious grace. Those who sense these faults within themselves, or have them pointed out by others, will not need to doubt the reality of their gifts, but will have a salutary reminder that maturity of character is not the automatic accompaniment of a spiritual gift.

Secondly, there are Christians who become perplexed and distressed by their own lack of special endowments. We have already emphasized that God is the sovereign Giver, and that His gifts are not to be contrasted and compared with a view to exalting some and disparaging others. We must now add that the cultivation of true Christlike character is more to be desired and more to be sought in prayer than the exercise of striking talents. A 'less gifted' Christian is not necessarily a less gracious Christian.

Thirdly, the warning and example of the Corinthian church should save us from too rash conclusions about any charismatic movement. Some Christians, aware of faults and excesses in such movements, immediately dismiss the whole thing as unworthy of serious thought. Lacking love as seriously as those we have already considered, they retail a few stories of excesses or mistakes, of unwise words and ungracious behaviour. 'There you are!' they say; 'the whole thing is delusion and nonsense!' But the gifts exercised in Corinth were not delusive nonsense, though the faults at Corinth were probably more grave than any we are likely to meet today. Their exercise was simply mixed with the intrusive influences of human weakness and human prejudice. Every undeniable work of God amongst His people has been to a greater or lesser extent spoiled and compromised by the failings of the Christians involved.

Perhaps Scripture's sternest warning to those who would measure spirituality by the presence or absence of gifts comes in Jesus' words in the Sermon on the Mount: 'Not every one who says to me, "Lord, Lord," shall enter the kingdom of heaven, but he who does the will of my Father who is in heaven. On that day many will say to me, "Lord, Lord, did we not prophesy in your name, and cast out demons in your name, and do many mighty works in your name?" And then will I declare to them, "I never knew you; depart from me, you evildoers"' (Mt. 7: 21–23). 'You will know them by their fruits' (Mt. 7: 16) said Jesus, and it is the fruit of the Spirit ('love, joy, peace, patience, kindness, goodness, faithfulness, gentleness, self-control' – Gl. 5: 22, 23), not the gifts of the Spirit, which indicates spirituality.

A false monopoly of truth

If the view we are examining is correct, and the gift of tongues is the required authentication of a necessary second experience of the Spirit, another conclusion necessarily follows: only those Christians who have had such an experience are really at the centre of God's will. All others have failed to grasp a fundamental part of God's revelation to His people. At least they are missing God's best for them: at worst they are closing their minds to His revealed purposes. Any attempt to exercise spiritual gifts outside the framework of the baptism of the Spirit will have little or no prospect of success, and apparent success in that field must be viewed with suspicion.

Now many Christians who teach the baptism of the Spirit would, of course, shrink from such conclusions. Many of them are gracious men and women who hold their beliefs in love and recognize that other Christians, who are faithfully following their Lord and who are being effectively used by Him in service, are sincere in feeling that they cannot share their views. With such as these no-one can have any quarrel. Indeed, as we shall show in the next chapter, we believe they have gained an important insight into an aspect of experience which often occurs in the lives of many, though not all, Christians; it is just that they are using inaccurate theological language in their attempt to explain this aspect of experience.

If a group of Christians becomes convinced that a post-conversion baptism of the Spirit evidenced by speaking in tongues is God's plan for all believers and the only gateway to blessing, then the worst of the attitudes towards other Christians outlined above will surface. This, in fact, is what has often happened during the present century.

Equally, of course, it would be unfair to those who believe in the necessity for a baptism of the Spirit after conversion to accuse them of being the only group of Christians who believe they have gained a true insight into scriptural truth where all others have failed. Groups of Christians, large and small, claiming a monopoly of truth and excommunicating all others with whom they cannot agree, have been around for the past nineteen centuries and are still with us today. Evangelical Christians particularly have a sad record here and many have still much to learn of the activity of God in denominational traditions other than their own.

One of the most exciting aspects of the current scene lies in the appearance of spiritual gifts among groups of Christians who traditionally have largely ignored or even opposed their exercise. It is also particularly significant that in many cases where this is happening little connection is being made between the gifts and traditional baptism of the Spirit theology. Thus, for many years, the Evangelical Lutheran Sisters of Mary in Darmstadt, Germany, have enjoyed a full-orbed experience of the gifts. Yet in her book, *Ruled by the Spirit*,[1] which deals in detail with these gifts, Basilea Schlink maintains that their exercise is the result of a constant attitude of repentance and love. The personal testimonies, which close the book, speak, not of a sudden crisis, but of a growing and deepening experience of the gifts and the fruit of the Spirit, preceded and accompanied by a real conflict with unbelief, timidity, selfishness and lovelessness within their own hearts.

In somewhat similar, although more theological, vein, another German Lutheran, Arnold Bittlinger, has reasoned in his commentary on 1 Corinthians 12-14,[2] that gifts should be exercised in the modern church. The writer assumes that all Christians are by definition baptized into the body of Christ, and are therefore potentially qualified to exercise spiritual gifts.

Turning from modern to less recent times it is again significant that, when charismatic phenomena have appeared at various times in church history, these have rarely been within the context of second-experience baptism of the Spirit teaching. When the early Fathers made reference to spiritual gifts, which they did from time to time, they did not differentiate between two grades of Christians. Similarly, the Montanist movement of the second century exercised spiritual gifts, yet does not seem to have taught the necessity of a second experience.

Quite clearly the early missionary activities of Saxon Christianity were strongly charismatic in nature. Confrontation with pagan priests, the healing of the sick, exorcism and miraculous deliverance from danger, were all regular experiences. During the Reformation Martin

[1] Basilea Schlink, *Ruled by the Spirit*. Translated from the German by J. Foote (Lakeland Publishers, 1970).
[2] A. Bittlinger, *Gifts and Graces*. Translated from the German by H. Klassen (Hodder and Stoughton, 1968).

Luther was said to have exercised all the gifts of the Spirit. The Anabaptist movement of the sixteenth century, once disowned and reviled, but now increasingly recognized as a spiritual ancestor of English-speaking Free Church Christianity, was a charismatic movement. Yet none of these had a post-conversion theology of the baptism of the Spirit.

This brief summary gives a salutary reminder that no single Christian group or tradition has a monopoly of understanding or practice in any area of New Testament teaching. The Spirit of God is not bound. He displays His activity sometimes in the most unlikely of places. Surely the history of reformation and revival illustrates this. This does not mean that apparently spiritual phenomena are more important than matters of belief or doctrine. The absolutely crucial test of any claim to Spirit-guided activity is the test of Scripture. The Holy Spirit in experience cannot contradict the Holy Spirit in the Bible. Judged by that test, some movements will be rejected as spurious. With others we may have to reserve judgment until their fruit becomes more apparent. Others we will gladly recognize as bearing the marks of a true work of God.

11 THE BAPTISM OF THE SPIRIT IN CHRISTIAN EXPERIENCE

In view of the hesitations felt by many Christians towards a post-conversion baptism of the Spirit, what is to be said of the claims made by many of new blessing in their lives following such an experience and its association with speaking in tongues? Such claims are frequent among certain groups of Christians, and indeed their fruitfulness in evangelism, their sterling missionary activity, the rapid growth of some of their churches and the quality of many of their lives in the areas of personal devotion and holiness cannot be gainsaid. Many readers of this book may well be in the habit of recalling two distinct experiences in their Christian lives, the first being their conversion when they first came to Christ and trusted Him for salvation, and the second, their 'baptism of the Spirit' from which they can honestly trace real progress. Are such claims and experiences to be dismissed as the fond illusions of misguided, if sincere, folk or do they reflect something which is very real in the experience of many Christians?

It is obvious that what some Christians refer to as their baptism with the Spirit is in fact, not a second experience, but a first, their conversion. If a Christian says that his baptism with the Spirit has resulted in his believing and enjoying the Bible in a new way, in his rejoicing in the nearness of Christ, in his witnessing to others without shame, in his finding freedom in prayer, in his experiencing the personal guidance of God, *etc.*, then it is fair to ask whether, before the 'baptism', the individual was a real Christian at all, for all these things are the mark of a Christian. It is quite possible that such a person may have been drawn to Christ in some way and may even have made some sort of partial response to His claims without having been truly born again in the New Testament sense of the word. There is ample evidence that some Christians' regeneration comes only after months, or even years, of groping and searching after Christ. If a 'baptism of the Spirit' of this nature is accompanied by spiritual gifts, including maybe speaking with tongues, that is fair enough. There is ample warrant for this from Scripture, as we have shown, as long as the individual concerned does not then demand that everybody else's experience of conversion should follow the precise pattern of his own.

Again, it is obvious that, when some Christians speak of having been 'baptized with the Spirit', they are referring to an experience which ended for them a period of coldness and backsliding. That they began to pray in tongues at this time proves nothing beyond the fact that, when they returned to the Lord, God first taught them this form of Christian prayer. The mistake lies in demanding tongues from all others and judging them second-class Christians if their experience does not tally with their own.

With others a so-called experience of 'baptism with the Spirit' refers to a time when they made rapid progress in the Christian life. Few Christians progress steadily in Christian growth throughout their lives. Many do have a second experience in which Christ becomes more real to them than He was before. Many have third and fourth and many subsequent experiences which all form part of their total Christian lives. Because speaking with tongues is one form of spiritual prayer it will not be surprising if its beginning coincides with such a second or subsequent experience. Some may begin to speak with tongues after prayerfully reconsidering the scriptures explained in this book. This will simply mean they will have begun to exercise a spiritual gift which God in His wisdom and sovereignty has made available to them. On the other hand there will be others who will go through their Christian lives and will never speak in tongues. So long as they exercise some of the gifts (and not necessarily the startling or extraordinary ones) they need have no fear that they are less complete because of this than their Christian friends who do, nor that in some mysterious way they are thereby missing God's best. 'There are varieties of gifts but the same Spirit.' 'All these are inspired by one and the same Spirit, who apportions to each one individually *as he wills*' (1 Cor. 12: 4, 11).

With yet others a so-called 'baptism of the Spirit' experience may coincide with a point in their spiritual lives at which they were empowered in a specific way for some particular kind of service. Such experiences, sometimes but not always accompanied by speaking with tongues, do seem to have occurred in the lives of Christians who later became particularly outstanding and effective.

George Whitefield, for example, already converted and widely recognized as a powerful preacher, shared an experience with the Wesley brothers in which the room was filled with a sense of God's glory. They were all cast to the ground, and were overwhelmed with a sensation of new power. The experience marked the beginning of a great surge forward in the Evangelical Awakening. William Tennant, a Presbyterian minister in the United States and a contemporary of Whitefield's, had a similar experience one night and awoke 'like a lion'. His preaching was henceforth mightily effective for a number of years, after which the experience left him as sharply and as decisively as it came.

D. L. Moody has recorded the incident when wave upon wave of divine energy came upon him until he had to ask God to desist. It was the beginning of his greatest work as an evangelist. John Pollock has made it very clear in his biography of Billy Graham that that evangelist had particularly meaningful experiences both before his first city-wide crusade in Los Angeles in 1949, and again before his crusade at Harringay, London, in 1954. Both these crusades marked new and increasingly influential stages in his ministry. Similar experiences to these have no doubt been recorded in the lives of many more Christians, known and unknown. It would be foolish to deny their reality and validity.

Since such men as those we have instanced have to endure temptations of pride and demagogy quite outside the experience of the vast majority of Christians because of their inevitable place in the public limelight, it is hardly surprising that the experiences which precede their anointing often involve a deep sense of unworthiness followed by a joyful new understanding of the work of Christ on their behalf. This is God's way of protecting them from the strains and pressures which will become theirs. It really is very dangerous when encouraging Christians to enter more fully into Christian experience and service to quote such instances as examples of what can follow from renewed vows of dedication for, of course, such startling results follow only in a tiny number of cases. If all are encouraged to expect such fruitfulness as a result of their experience many are likely to be discouraged and disillusioned when the promised fruit does not materialize, and some may give up the Christian life altogether.

Although all true Christian experience must begin with new birth, the way to new birth, the means of new birth and the results of new birth will vary enormously from individual to individual. For some the new birth experience will be a highly dramatic and emotional crisis in their lives, a moment which they will be able to pinpoint for the rest of their days. With others new birth will be much quieter and less spectacular. Still others will be unable to mark the moment of their new birth, but will only be able to say, 'One thing I know, that though I was blind, now I see' (Jn. 9: 25).

Equally, Christian life after new birth will vary enormously from Christian to Christian. Some will make rapid and dramatic progress and may reach a position of leadership in the church and become well known. Others will follow Christ much more quietly and unobtrusively. Some will make only halting and faltering progress for many years; spiritual maturity will take a long time to achieve. Some will have a 'second experience' which overnight will transform a hitherto weak and ineffective witness. Others will have several crucial experiences subsequent to their conversion. Some will exercise dramatic and startling spiritual gifts. Others will exercise less obtrusive yet equally fruitful and necessary gifts. Quite clearly none will reach a position this side of heaven in which new discoveries of the power and influence of the Holy Spirit are not needed!

It is our contention that what many Christians may *call* a 'baptism of the Spirit' is in fact an experience which comes into one of these categories which we have listed. There can be no scriptural objection to any of these, for none of them implies that regeneration is an incomplete work of the Holy Spirit, and none of them divides Christians into two distinct categories in an unscriptural manner. Some writers do indeed recognize that in what many Christians call a baptism of the Spirit experience they are simply appropriating more of what potentially became theirs at their conversion and the difference between their position and that taken by this book is very small indeed. For example, Larry Christenson, who in some places seems to teach two distinct experiences, nevertheless goes on to say, 'The baptism with the Holy Spirit is a specific link in a chain of experiences which unites a believer to Christ. The chain has three links: repentance and faith, water baptism and baptism with the Holy Spirit. . . . The normal sequence seems to have no significant time lapse. For all practical purposes it is one unified experience, with three distinct aspects.'[1] He goes on to suggest (as we have done) that the stories in Acts which reveal a different pattern are recorded precisely for that purpose; they are interesting exceptions for special reasons.

[1] Larry Christenson, *Speaking in Tongues and its Significance for the Church* (Fountain Trust, 1968).

Christians of all traditions must constantly be on their guard against the temptation to force the experiences of others into a pattern which conforms with their own, however valuable and meaningful for them those experiences may have been. This has been very much one of the besetting sins of evangelical Christians in modern times. Such dogmatism as to the precise form of experience through which all Christians must pass dishonours God by its refusal to recognize the infinite varieties of human nature, and can lead only to bitterness and division as individuals rightly reject such spiritual totalitarianism. 'There are varieties of working, but it is the same God who inspires them all in every one' (1 Cor. 12: 6).

III APPROPRIATING SPIRITUAL GIFTS

12 THE BENEFITS OF SPIRITUAL GIFTS

The divine origin and importance of spiritual gifts has generally been recognized throughout the history of the Christian church. The study of the Scriptures by Christians has ensured that this has been so. What has not always been recognized is the theology of the church as the body of Christ which lies behind spiritual gifts, and the continuing importance and relevance of the exercise of all the gifts. When these have been lost then the church has been impoverished, for Christians have not then sought to enter into all the blessings that God has for them. It is our conviction that when churches consciously seek to operate as the body of Christ, with all their members between ther. willing to exercise all the gifts, then certain benefits will follow.

An awakening and mobilizing of church memberships

One result of willingness to exercise spiritual gifts will be an awakening and mobilizing of church memberships. Is not the normal view of the church today that of a religious corporation employing clergy to work, and inviting laity to come along? This is not the Bible view. The Bible views the church as a body with every member vital to its functioning, and with a necessary part to play for the benefit of all. The Acts of the Apostles paints a picture of churches in which everybody was involved, in worship, in service and in evangelism. Those who received Peter's word on the day of Pentecost 'devoted themselves . . . to the breaking of bread and the prayers' (Acts 2: 41, 42) – the church at worship. 'All who believed . . . sold their possessions and goods and distributed them to all, as any had need' (Acts 2: 44, 45) – the church in service. Those who were scattered from Jerusalem following the death of Stephen went about preaching the Word, some to Jews and some to Gentiles (Acts 8: 4; 11: 19, 20) – the church in evangelism. Recognition of the true nature of the church today and of the obligation of all Christians to exercise various gifts should bring stagnant congregations to life as every member seeks to play his part in the strengthening of the community.

A powerful witness

Churches with awakened and mobilized membership exercising spiritual gifts are churches whose witness is powerful. Exercise of the gift of healing on the lame man at the Beautiful Gate of the Temple led to a series of events which brought the membership of the Jerusalem Christian community up to five thousand (Acts 4: 4) and silenced the opposition and cynicism of the Jewish leaders (Acts 4: 14). Exercise of the gift of contribution in liberality coincided with the great power with which the apostles were able to testify to the resurrection (Acts 4: 33). Exercise of the gift of knowledge in the matter of Ananias' and Sapphira's deception again led to a series of incidents which culminated in 'multitudes both of men and women' benefiting from the ministry of the church (Acts 5: 12–16). Exercise of the gift of martyrdom on the part of Stephen led to an extension of Christian witness into Judea, Samaria, Phoenicia, Cyprus and Antioch. The hallmark of this early Christian evangelism was its authority. Opponents could not withstand the wisdom and the Spirit with which the Christians spoke (see Acts 6: 10). Of course the common feature in each incident was the preaching and teaching. At Lystra, indeed, the miraculous healing of the lame man was seriously misunderstood until it was put firmly in its context of preaching (Acts 14: 8–18). Nevertheless, the writer of Acts clearly implies that the exercise of various gifts attracted interest in the gospel's message and powerfully confirmed the gospel's claims. So today, we should expect that, when the church is mobilized and gifts are exercised, then it will be powerful in its witness to others.

Spirit-filled leadership

An emphasis on spiritual gifts within a worshipping community should further lead to the appointment of Spirit-filled leaders. It is a striking fact that personality and intellect seem to have taken a minor place in the qualities required of leaders in the New Testament churches. Moral and spiritual qualities were given priority. Faced with the need for better administration of welfare work, the apostles said, 'Pick out from among you seven men of good repute, full of the Spirit and of wisdom' (Acts 6: 3). 'Now in the church at Antioch there were prophets and teachers. . . . The Holy Spirit said, "Set apart for me Barnabas and Saul for the work to which I have called them." Then after fasting and praying they laid their hands on them and sent them off' (Acts 13: 1–3). The qualifications required of church leaders in the Pastoral Epistles illustrate the same point (1 Tim. 3 and 4). Naturally one would expect that a community which valued the enabling of the Holy Spirit would require leaders who displayed such enabling in their own lives. The leaders in turn would continue to depend on divine help rather than natural ability.

It is a point which needs to be continually underlined. As any denomination or organization becomes well established and more conscious of the society in which it lives, it becomes increasingly liable to look for qualities in its leaders similar to those sought in secular organizations. The response to spiritual crisis, failure in evangelism, confrontation with new situations, is often to appoint leaders who have what seem to be the natural qualifications. People are better educated, so leaders must be academically better equipped. The image of the church is poor, so a good public relations man is needed. Young people are not being touched, so a visual-aids expert must be brought in. Television is the commonest means of communication, so a photogenic personality would be useful. Small churches are losing ground, so an expert on reorganization is required. None of this is wrong in itself. The service of Christ demands the best. Spirituality does not mean academic poverty or slipshod organization. Nevertheless the emphasis can be dangerous. The New Testament church required of its leaders qualities that were predominantly spiritual and moral.

Recent developments in some parts of the world once designated 'foreign mission-fields' have strikingly demonstrated that Spirit-filled leadership can emerge rapidly when God is freely at work. Persecution or political changes have compelled missionaries to leave areas where they had laboured for many years. Half-trained indigenous leaders have had to take control and immediately deal with crisis-situations. The need for Spirit-anointed leadership has been drastically demonstrated. And in the crisis, God has not failed His people. At the end of a time of persecution the indigenous church has emerged stronger than ever.

In more sophisticated countries the same truth has been underlined. Few Christians will have difficulty in thinking of some local leader who lacks formal theological qualifications. Yet his work has been crowned with success, sometimes amongst those groups hardest to reach with the gospel, the working-class, immigrants, modern youth. Side by side with him, of course, is the frequent example of the highly-qualified servant of God with his intellect, personality and disciplined training dedicated to God, and the anointing of the Holy Spirit on his ministry. But the feature which both have in common is spiritual power. It is a spiritual conflict in which Christians are engaged, and 'the weapons of our warfare are not worldly but have divine power to destroy strongholds' (2 Cor. 10: 4). John Bunyan the pot-mender and Gladys Aylward the parlour-maid are constant reminders of that.

Closer integration

A further result of the exercise of spiritual gifts should surely be a deepening of unity within the church and amongst all Christian groups. The New Testament repeatedly insists that this is one of their purposes, that individually-endowed believers should act and react together like the variously-endowed links of a human body. Clearly this is not always happening, and we have suggested some reasons why. No group has a monopoly of the faults in that situation. Nevertheless there are enough happy examples available to demonstrate in practice what the Scriptures expect. When members of a local congregation recognize their mutual interdependence they are drawn closer together in fellowship and love. When they understand the equal value in God's sight of their varied abilities they more eagerly work together for the common good. When they appreciate that their different gifts are not yet another example of the general unfairness of life, but rather an essential ingredient in God's wise plan, they readily co-operate in the forwarding of God's work. Occasions of jealousy and bickering are set in perspective. So much work cries out to be done that there is little energy left for back-biting and rivalry. This may seem idealistic; but when the Bible gives such a pattern, dare it be called unrealistic?

Deeper experience of worship

Besides all these benefits the exercise of gifts within Christian communities should lead them into a deeper experience of worship. Earlier in this book attention was drawn to the informal nature of worship in the church at Corinth as compared with most worship in our own day. The point was made that such worship was not the only form of worship practised in the early church, but that liturgical worship was practised as well. It was suggested that there is a place for both kinds of worship in any balanced Christian community. At a time when established liturgies are undergoing revision and when exciting experiments are being conducted in the quest for more meaningful and relevant forms of worship, this is worth bearing in mind.

Thus churches which recognize gifts need not abandon cherished liturgical forms and set prayers in order that they may be exercised. They can use both programmed and spontaneous forms of worship and their gatherings can be enriched as a result. Indeed, revolution in worship, abandoning long-accepted forms and replacing them with prophecies, tongues and the like, might only do more harm than good and bring gifts into the kind of disrepute they quickly suffered at the beginning of the century. Each case, of course, must be judged on its merits, but at the present time, in churches unused to the exercise of gifts in worship, the house-meeting would seem to provide a particularly appropriate environment for charismatic worship. As long as such meetings are kept open and above-board, and as long as those who attend resist every temptation to form a holy huddle or to regard themselves as a super-spiritual clique, no harm need result. Indeed, it should go without saying that such house-meetings should always be openly advertised as part of the church's normal programme and whenever possible should be attended by the vicar or minister.

'Eye hath not seen, nor ear heard, neither have entered into the heart of man, the things which God hath prepared for them that love him. But God hath revealed them unto us by his Spirit' (1 Cor. 2: 9, 10, AV). These are exciting days in which to be a Christian. Churches find themselves no longer part of the Establishment but acting as minority groups in missionary situations. Christians are compelled to distinguish as never before between the essentials of the gospel and the traditional and social accretions that have been added to it. Often the gauntlet of outright challenge is thrown down by militant unbelief. Followers of Christ are surrounded by non-Christian people who are puzzled by their divisions and unimpressed by their claim to have God's love poured into their hearts (Rom. 5: 5). Within the churches are those who would empty the gospel of any supernatural content. The good news is defined in terms of human social action. Fellowship with God is simply an expression for human neighbourliness. Prayer means simply talk about reality. The church is supposed to have invisibility as its aim.

In large areas of the world determined and highly-organized persecution of the church has all the resources of a monolithic state at its disposal. Martyrdom has claimed as many Christians in the twentieth century as in the whole three-hundred-year conflict with the Roman Empire. Crude forces of animism and sophisticated resurgences of old hostile religions stand embattled against what are thought of in Europe and the USA as the 'overseas churches'.

Could it be that in these stirring and demanding days God is meeting the situation with a recall of His people to an awareness of their spiritual heritage? Could it be that many Christians have not reckoned as they should on the willingness of the Head of the church to give gifts to men for the strengthening, upbuilding and extension of His people? If this is so, and if the reappearance of long-neglected spiritual gifts is part of that recall and that reckoning, then their relevance at such a time is obvious. There is a crying need for a mobilized church to evangelize while there is time. There is a crying need for a powerful witness to convince the doubtful and silence the hostile. Spirit-filled leadership is more necessary than ever for demanding days. Communities of Christians must be bound together by love and must function in mutual trust. They need to meet with God in true, Spirit-led worship. They need to exercise all the gifts which God has given to His church.

13 SPIRITUAL GIFTS AND THE INDIVIDUAL CHRISTIAN

Throughout this book we have sought to set spiritual gifts within the context of the teaching of the whole of Scripture and this has involved us in setting them within the context of the church. Nevertheless some individual Christians may remain puzzled. Some may feel that they are completely lacking in gifts. Others, while aware that they have been equipped by God in certain ways, may find themselves longing to exercise other gifts. All may be wondering just how these spiritual gifts may be obtained.

We hope we have shown that it is through spiritual endowments that the Christian is enabled to serve his Lord, bring blessing to others and take his proper place in the life of the church. In the passages which have formed the basis of our study in this book (Rom. 12, 1 Cor. 12–14 and Eph. 4) it is always assumed that Christians already possess gifts. Rarely is it suggested that they should seek them. The main thrust of Paul's teaching is to show how the Christian should rightfully employ the gifts he has without any exaggerated ideas of his own importance (Rom. 12), but with a realization of the purpose of these gifts in God's order for the church (Eph. 4), and a genuine concern for the building up of God's people in an atmosphere of love (1 Cor. 12–14). We have seen that neither these passages nor the narrative-portions in Acts lay down a programme or a method of entering into the possession and exercise of gifts. There is no command to pursue a course of persistent or agonized searching for particular abilities.

All this, plus the additional fact that gifts are described as being distributed from the hand of a sovereign God who knows what we need before we ask Him, would seem to imply that the exercise of gifts is a spontaneous outworking of our Christian progress. Just as the fruit of the Spirit (love, joy, peace, *etc.*) appears in the normal course of Christian development as we walk in obedience to God's will and appropriate all that He offers to us rather than through deliberate concentration on one particular virtue, so we may expect the gifts of the Spirit to appear too. Situations will arise in our service to Christ, in which we need to act in a particular rôle. As long as we are not inhibited by nervousness, doubt, or unbelief, we may well expect that the appropriate response to the situation will become possible. If our experience is a dramatic one, we will not be misled into insisting that the sovereign Spirit works according to the same pattern in everyone else's life, nor will we then give more importance to a past experience than to a day-by-day progress.

The principles which govern progress in this direction are those which govern any other spiritual progress. The Christian should be regular in prayer and the study of the Scriptures, in attendance at worship at his local church and in participation in the Lord's Supper. He should constantly desire the working out of God's will for his life and should seek to be actively employed in some form of Christian service. In this context he can earnestly desire the spiritual gifts, and can rest in the promises of Christ, 'Ask, and it will be given you.... For every one who asks receives.... If you then, who are evil, know how to give good gifts to your children, how much more will the heavenly Father give the Holy Spirit to those who ask him!' (Lk. 11: 9–13).

Having come o such a position the Christian is reminded 'to rekindle the gift of God that is within you' (2 Tim. 1: 6). This he will do by remaining faithful and obedient to Christ in his everyday life, and active in the service to

158

which he has been called. It is thus our conviction that there is no short cut to the reception of spiritual gifts, nor any once-for-all experience in which they are permanently granted. Day-by-day discipleship is necessary to their continuation, and the parable of the slothful servant (Mt. 25: 14–30) remains a salutary warning to those who neglect God's gracious provision for us.

Perhaps most of all the individual Christian needs to remember that the Holy Spirit is sovereign, free, unpredictable, mysterious. He 'apportions to each one individually as he wills' (1 Cor. 12: 11). He raises up church officers to exercise certain rôles, anoints individuals to meet particular situations, directs seemingly natural abilities into channels of loving service, powerfully demonstrates divine intervention in critical situations, and enables Christians to accomplish deeds otherwise impossible.

He is still clearly at work today in all of these ways. New situations make new demands, and Christians can watch with reverent gratitude as new combinations and permutations of familiar gifts become possible. How can we classify the demonstrations of divine power which made Wycliffe and Hus the shining lights of a dark age? Were no gifts o the Spirit released in the Reformation through the skill of Bible translator and printer? Into what categories do the endowments of John Bunyan, Richard Baxter, Jonathan Edwards and David Brainerd fall? What precisely equipped Charles Simeon to influence untold numbers of students, and William Carey to blaze a trail of missionary enterprise? How can the work of Christian social reformers such as Wilberforce and Shaftesbury be classified? What was there about Charles Spurgeon and William Booth which lightened the gloom of Victorian London? Who equipped D. L. Moody and Brownlow North to be evangelists to the multitudes? What produced theologians like Cunningham or Hodge and martyrs like Bishop Hannington and the Ugandan Christians? Who empowered Martin Niemöller to defy a godless tyrant and Watchman Nee to influence a generation from prison? Where in the scale of spiritual gifts can we place the abilities of C. S. Lewis, and what precisely gives new hope and restored faith to thousands at L'Abri?

To distinguish between natural and supernatural is difficult in a world which is governed by the omnipotent and omnipresent God. To distinguish between the less colourful and the more dramatic expressions of His activity has little value. Christians need to recognize continually that the Holy Spirit is at work through those who believe and obey, and thus function as limbs in the body of Christ. They should recognize that what constitutes an activity as charismatic is its origin in the initiative of the Spirit and its exercise as an expression of the grace of God. In doing so, Christians will neither undervalue the quiet, undramatic work nor be childishly dazzled by the more spectacular. They will be careful of their motives in seeking certain gifts which they find personally attractive. They will have an attitude of expectation and confidence, believing in One who can and does marvellously meet the situation of the moment with His grace and power and who demonstrates that nothing is impossible with Him. They will rejoice when fellow-Christians are led into rôles which they have not filled and are enabled to exercise gifts which they themselves do not have. Since it is God who distributes the gifts out of the bounty of His grace there is no ultimate difference between those who exercise one gift and those who exercise another. Therefore all Christians can cry, 'Thanks be to God for his inexpressible gift!' (2 Cor. 9: 15).